Intimacy with God in Me

The Benefits of Living in the Secret Place with God

Maxine A. Ryan

Intimacy with God in Me: The Benefits of Living in the Secret Place with God
All rights reserved.
Copyright © 2021 by Maxine A. Ryan
Cover art copyright© 2021, Istock

P.O. Box 22
Clarksburg, Maryland 20871
Email: Maxineryan48@gmail.com

ISBN: 978-1-7373080-0-3 (Hardcover Edition)
ISBN: 978-1-7373080-1-0 (Ebook Edition)

Library of Congress Control Number: 2021911354

No part of this publication may be reproduced, stored in a retrieval system, or transmitted in any form or by any means electronic, mechanical, photocopying, recording, or any otherwise without the written permission of the author or publisher.

Italicized in text are scriptures from the Holy Bible.

Verses that are without a reference are taking from the King James Version of the Bible. All rights reserved.

Verses marked AMP are taken from the Amplified Bible AMP, Copyright © 2015 by The Lockman Foundation, La Habra, CA 90631. All rights reserved. http//wwwlockman.org

Verses marked NKJV are taken from the New King James Version Bible, Copyright © 1982 by Thomas Nelson, All rights reserved.

Verses marked ERV are taken from the Easy-to -Read Version Copyright © 1987, 2004 Bible League International. All rights reserved.

Verses marked TPT are taken from the Passion Translation ® is a registered trademark of Passion & Fire Ministries, Inc. Copyright © 2020 Passion & Fire Ministries, Inc. All rights reserved.

Verses marked NLT are taken from the New Living Translation Bible Copyright © 1996, 2004, 2007, 2015 by Tyndale House Foundation. All rights reserved.

Printed in the United States of America.

DEDICATION

To my dear grandmother Violda December, while you were here with us, your demonstration of intimacy with the Father truly captured my heart. I am truly honored and thankful for your life and your example, Granny. Thank you for your sacrificial and selfless life of prayer. You prayed for your family—also for anyone who came in contact with you. Granny, I thank you for building an altar of prayer and leaving us with a rich legacy of prayer in our hearts. My heart is grateful for all you have given me. You have given me something money cannot buy! You have given me Jesus! You are still an inspiration to me, and I am grateful to God to be your granddaughter. Dearest grandmother, I dedicate this book to you. I love you!

Table of Contents

Dedication iii

My Love Letter to Abba Father vi

Introduction viii

Chapter 1: Intimacy Builds Altars 1

Chapter 2: The Holy Spirit Draws Believers Into Intimacy 28

Chapter 3: The Secret Place Revealed 48

Chapter 4: Waiting for the Lord 54

Chapter 5: Prayer: The Most Important Conversation of the Day 59

Chapter 6: Fasting Is Intimacy 89

Chapter 7: Supernatural Encounter Through Intimacy 109

Chapter 8: Releasing the Anointing and Presence of God 120

Chapter 9: Overflow of His Presence 137

Chapter 10: Discovering the Inner You 145

Chapter 11: Intimacy Gives Us the Ability to Be Bold 159

Chapter 12: Intimacy Positions Us to Hear God's Voice 172

Chapter 13: Intimacy Positions the Overcomer 196

Chapter 14: The Believer Bears Fruit in the Secret Place........... 208

Chapter 15: Intimacy Allows Us to Leave a Legacy 214

Acknowledgements 227

My Love Letter to Abba Father

To the only wise God, the one who is and is to come. Jehovah Shammah, the God who is always there. You knew me before you formed me in my mother's womb. You loved me even when I was not thinking about you. For this, I will forever love you. As the psalmist wrote in Psalm 63, I thirst for you in this dry and weary land without water. I have seen you in every season of my life. I have seen your strength and glory. Your faithful love is better than life itself, so my lips will praise you all the days of my life. In your name, I will lift my hands in prayer.

When I sit in your presence, you satisfy my hunger. My joyful lips hunger to praise you! I remember you while lying on my bed and when I am rising. Abba, you are the first thing I think about in the morning; you are on my mind during the day and in the middle of the night. You are the one who helps, restores, comforts, and loves me. I am happy to be under your protection! I will stay close to you for the rest of my days because you uphold me with your powerful arm. I wrote this book as a token of my love for you. I desire to share with the world how much you and our time together means to me. You have filled my life with the joy of your presence. I love you, my Savior and my Lord!

Yours Truly,

Maxine

INTRODUCTION

When God created the first man, Adam, He created him to live in fellowship with Him. Yet God said it was not right for man to be alone. Then, God created Eve to be Adam's help-meet and walk alongside him (Genesis 2:18). God intended for her to be *intimate* with him —so that they could be fruitful, multiply, replenish and subdue the earth. Adam could not do these things on his own. Even the animals had this assignment; they were created male and female for the purpose of reproduction.

After Adam and Eve ate from the tree of the knowledge of good and evil, Genesis 3:8 says, *They heard the voice of the LORD God walking in the garden in the cool of the day: and Adam and his wife hid themselves from the presence of the LORD God amongst the trees of the garden. And the LORD God called unto Adam, and said unto him, Where art thou?*

There is a problem with these two verses. Adam and Eve were created to commune with God; however, they were hiding from God. For the first time in their lives, they were out of fellowship with God because of their sin. Sin put a wedge between God and man. Nevertheless, Jesus, the second "Adam" (1 Corinthians 15:22), restored the union between God and man. Man became the carrier of God's presence through Jesus Christ. Man did not have to be ashamed or distance himself from God anymore.

When believers fellowship (Greek word for fellowship is *koinonia,* which means communion, joint participation, or intimacy) with God, it is not about twisting God's arm to get what we want. Fellowship is having a personal relationship. Also, this fellowship with God is not about works or our own effort like it was under the old covenant. Through the cross, what Jesus accomplished placed us under a far better covenant than the one established with the children of Israel. Believers today are no longer distant from God nor do we have to do works to gain access to Him. Believers have the Holy Spirit within, who draws us into intimacy with the Father because of Jesus' perfect sacrifice.

When we received Jesus as our personal Savior, *every spiritual blessing in the heavenly realm has already been lavished upon us as a love gift from our wonderful heavenly Father, the Father of our Lord Jesus—all because he sees us wrapped into Christ* (Ephesians 1:3, TPT). Therefore, when we are intimate with God, we are responding to the drawing of the Holy Spirit and to God's love extended to us through intimacy.

Moreover, the kind of intimacy God desires is free will. It is birthed out of relationship, not works or self-effort. As a matter of fact, instead of praying and fasting for ten hours in our own strength trying to get God to move, we believe in what the finished work of the cross has already made available. We rely on the Holy Spirit to lead us and direct our steps. We ask the Holy Spirit how long we should fast and pray, we are *one* with Him.

We are literally imitating the relationship Jesus has with the Father. Jesus is one with His Father and lived a life of intimacy. He released miracles, signs, and wonders.

When we are plugged into the source of life, which is God, all things that seem impossible become possible. We live life in the supernatural, the same way Jesus did. Furthermore intimacy with God keeps the fire burning in *and* through us. Our relationship with God is not mechanical and boring. It is based on love and affection. Having daily communion with God keeps the fire burning afresh in our hearts for Him. If we neglect our pursuit of intimacy, our fire goes dim.

The same principle can be applied to marriage. The flames of intimacy burn tremendously during the beginning stages of the relationship. As the years pass, the flames of romance grow dim. The husband and wife do not pursue each other in their marriage. They do not take the time to invest. The marriage becomes mechanical and ultimately, they part ways. If only they had taken the time to *fan the flames*, and rekindle the romance they once had, it could have been saved. Hence, I thank God that He will always be with us, so we can *always* rekindle our intimacy with Him.

Intimacy with God is important. It not only keeps our flames burning; it makes us fruitful, powerful, and bold as a lion. In the process we build a godly altar that will last forever. Prayer is an important part of our relationship; this is how we communicate with the Father. Nothing happens in this earth apart from prayer. Prayer is the *most* important conversation a person can have. It gives God access to the earth.

The Bible says in 2 Peter 1:3 (TPT), *everything we could ever need for life and godliness has already been deposited in us by his divine power. For all this was lavished upon us through the rich experience of knowing him who has called us by his name and invited us to come to him through a glorious manifestation of his goodness.* So, we have already been loaded with everything we need for living a godly life. Prayer is one vehicle that positions us to move what is given to us in the spirit to the natural world.

If you desire deeper levels of power and intimacy with God through Christ, then this book is for you. I will share some benefits pertaining to intimacy with God, along with how intimacy positions us for encounters with the Father. You will learn why I believe it is important to sit in the face of God daily. How I grew spiritually because of *intimacy* with God in me. Finally, where you can find God's power and why intimacy gives believers an ear to hear. We will also discuss how intimacy with God positions a believer to be an overcomer, and why the enemy tries his best to distract us from sitting in the secret place. After reading this book, you will desire more from the Lord!

The words on these pages bring no glory to me, the author. Every testimony, encounter and revelation comes from God. To Him, *all* the glory belongs. Nothing God gives us can be earned through prayer and fasting. It is by pure, unselfish love that He has favored and rewarded us. When we have encounters with Him, it is by grace that He chooses to do what He pleases. As you read, I pray you will receive an impartation that changes your life from this day forward. And that God will stir up the gifts within, and you will experience the tangible glory of His presence. *I pray that you will continually experience the immeasurable greatness of God's power made available to you through faith. Then your life will be an advertisement of this immense power as it works through you!* (Ephesians 1:19, TPT). This is in the mighty and powerful name of Jesus. Amen!

Chapter 1

Intimacy Builds Altars

WHEN A BELIEVER'S PRAYER LIFE is constant, altars are built. Altars are gateways to the supernatural world—either to heaven or hell—according to Genesis 28:17. Throughout the Old Testament, the Israelites built altars to God and offered sacrifices on the altars. Many great men and women like Solomon, built many evil shrines (altars) to worship false gods (1 Kings 11:7–8). There are many [different] kinds of altars. In this book, we will talk about godly altars, ancestral altars, and demonic family altars.

The Hebrew word for altar is *mizbeach*; the root word is *zabach*, which means to slaughter, kill, and sacrifice or to slaughter for sacrifice. According to the Merriam-Webster dictionary, an *altar* is a [usually] raised structure on which sacrifices are offered, or incense is burned. To offer God a perfect sacrifice on the altar—one pleasing to Him—means that our carnality must die.

According to 1 Corinthians 1:29 (AMP), *...no one may [be able to] boast in the presence of the God. All of the glory belongs to Him; none belongs to us.*

People build altars to commune with a deity. It is a place of sacrifice, worship, covenant, remembrance, and power. It is a place of exchange, cleansing, and birthing. Under the old covenant, wood, stone, and fire sacrifices were necessary for an altar. The Israelites were required to offer their best flock to God. If the animal sacrificed had any imperfections, or was not young, God rejected it. The sons of Aaron, Nadab and Abihu offered *strange* fire on the altar. Both lost their lives for not following God's directions (Leviticus 10). The sacrifices of the Old Testament represented Christ, who would later be offered on the cross as the ultimate and perfect sacrifice for mankind.

Now, Abraham had great faith. He was willing to give God his best offer—his son, Isaac—as a sacrificial offering. He believed God many years for the child of promise. Then, God tested his faith. God told Abraham to take Isaac up to Mount Moriah, build an altar to Him and offer his son (Genesis 22).

One thing I love about Abraham is how he trusted God with his whole life. He was willing to give something valuable and precious to him. This sacrifice would have cost Abraham the descendants God promised him. But it did not matter to Abraham.

He knew God and trusted Him to fulfill every promise made to him and his seed.

In Revelation 8:3–4 (NLT), the Bible says, *Then, another angel with a gold incense burner came and stood at the altar. And a great amount of incense was given to him to mix with the prayers of God's people as an offering on the gold altar before the throne. The smoke of the incense, mixed with the prayers of God's holy people, ascended up to God from the altar where the angel had poured them out.* Once a believer prays on earth, incense is mixed with our prayers and goes up before God as an offering. And the fire on the altar burns as sweet-smelling incense. The offering is given as part of worship and sacrifice. When the believer has little or no intimacy with God, the fire goes dim. The fire is not completely out since we have the Holy Spirit living inside of us. However, it was different for the Israelites—they did not have the Holy Spirit living on the inside of them. They had no fire.

One example can be seen in the life of Eli. Although he was a priest of the Lord, he had no flame burning on the inside (1 Samuel). I concluded that Eli did not fear God because of his hardened heart. Eli's sons held God's offering in contempt, and God warned Eli He would put them away in death. Eli ignored several warnings the Lord gave to him (1 Samuel 2:12-36).

On the other hand, David was a man after God's heart. This was a foreshadow of the Holy Spirit living in man. He had an intimate relationship with God, lived a life of repentance even though David had sinned against God. The Bible says, he slept with Bathsheba and impregnated her. And he [unsuccessfully] tried to cover it up (2 Samuel 2:11) by calling her husband Uriah home from the battlefield to sleep with Bathsheba to conceal the true paternity. When Uriah refused, David commanded Joab to send Uriah to the front line of the fiercest battle. Uriah was killed. Once the period of mourning was complete, David brought Bathsheba in his home to become his wife (2 Samuel 11). Although, David thought he had gotten away with this, God sent Nathan the prophet to rebuke him (2 Samuel 12). After the rebuke, David repented. Every time we read Psalm 51, we are reminded of what David said to God. Eli and David both lived during the time of the old covenant. The difference was David feared God.

The angel of the Lord told the prophet Gad to tell David to build an altar before Him on the threshing floor of Araunah, the Jebusite. Araunah wanted to give David the threshing floor. David told him he would prefer to pay full price and he refused to present an offering to God that cost him nothing (2 Samuel 24:22). David built an altar through prayer. He reverenced God, which is why God said David was a man after His heart (Acts 13:22).

We can learn from David that an offering [intimacy] the believer presents to God on their altar should be a sacrificial one, given from a heart of love. It must cost us something and be the best of what we have. Giving God leftovers is *not* our best. We see this from the beginning when Cain and Abel presented their offerings to God—He rejected Cain's leftover offering. Abel gave God the [best] firstlings of his flock (Genesis 4:3-4, ERV). The Lord accepted Abel's offering, which came from his heart; he put God first.

Today, the fire of God burns in the hearts of believers. Believers who have a constant prayer life, fear God, easily come to repentance—and are sensitive to the Holy Spirit's voice. We are carriers of God's glory. And believers shift atmospheres that are not conducive to what we believe.

Throughout the old covenant, God's fire was foreshadow of an actual altar made with wood, stone, and other required ceremonial materials. When the people set up altars, God showed up and lit the fire. He indeed is a consuming fire (Hebrews 12:29). Moreover this fire is God [Himself] that burns on the inside of the believer, and the flames get hotter through intimacy! Each believer is responsible for keeping their *own* fire burning by spending time in God's presence. Therefore, our best offering is required as we build an altar of prayer to God.

The contest between Elijah and the prophets of Baal on Mount Carmel is a representation of God's fire and power. The altar of the Lord was erected, and it was time for offering and sacrifices. Elijah prayed to the God of Abraham, Isaac, and Jacob.

When he finished praying, immediately the fire of the Lord flashed down from heaven— burned up the young bull, the wood, the stone, and the dust. It even licked up all the water in the trench (1 Kings 18:36–38). It was God who answered by fire in the midst of a showdown.

Gideon, who was a judge of Israel, encounters God answering by fire (Judges 6). An angel of the Lord appeared before Gideon and gave him instructions on how to build an altar (Judges 6:20). When Gideon did as he was told, *then the angel of the LORD touched the meat and bread with the tip of the staff in his hand, and fire flamed up from the rock and consumed all he had brought. And the angel of the Lord disappeared* (Judges 6:21, NLT).

The same way the children of Israel built altars to meet with God, altars are built for Satan to fellowship with people. During this fellowship, evil powers are received and covenants are made. Also, spells, exchanges, and evil birthing takes place. These altars can be seen in a temple, designated areas, or set up in homes as a shrine. When power, covenant, or spells are needed, an individual takes their sacrifice (animals, money, or anything of value) to a designated place to access the power of an evil altar.

One time, I received a prayer request from a young woman who has a high-paying job in the government. Because she has a degree, it made her income earnings high. When she was hired jealousy arose. A co-worker went to an evil altar, took a sacrifice, and made an exchange. The ritualist placed the name of the young woman on the altar and gave the co-worker something to drop in the young woman's food. The co-worker cooked a meal and dropped the substance in the food and fed it to the young woman. The young woman became extremely sick and her family thought she was not going to survive. She lost so much weight because she could not keep any food down. We prayed, broke the enemy's power and today this young woman is still alive to tell what God has done. Evil altars are real. Some people access them daily to communicate with evil.

Demonic altars of ancestors are inherited, meaning someone in the family previously made a covenant with Satan. Once inherited, their main purposes are to kill, steal and destroy lives. Any altar built outside of a covenant with God is evil, and it will block progress, cripple spiritual growth, destroy the fruits of our ground and prevent us from receiving our blessings from the Lord. Spiritually, the believer has already been blessed by God, but these ancestors' altars stop the individual from making the transfer from the spiritual to the natural world they live in. We can learn about evil ancestral altars from the story of Gideon in Judges 6.

Gideon's ancestors chose to turn their backs on their covenant with the God, to be in covenant with Baal. Even though Gideon's ancestors had built these altars of Baal, it was his responsibility to tear them down before God could use him. During his encounter with the Lord, God was cleaning away everything in Gideon's life that opposed Him. If Gideon had not destroyed his family's altar of Baal, it would have been passed onto his generations.

Here is an actual story of an ancestral altar. Alph Lukau, who is a renowned prophet and pastor from Alleluia Ministries International of South Africa, called out a woman from his congregation by her birthday and name. God had revealed her current pain to him. As she made her way to the front of the church, the Lord began revealing to him the evil covenant that was passed down to her from a family member when she was young. This woman's aunt was a witch and a wizard. Before she died, she needed to pass this altar to a *firstborn* in the family. This is alarming to me because of what the Lord says about the firstborn.

For all the firstborn are mine. When I struck down all the firstborn in Egypt, I set apart for myself every firstborn in Israel, whether human or animal. They are to be mine. I am the LORD (Numbers 3:13, NIV).

This is an example of how Satan imitates God. He tries to destroy the life of the firstborn —the first portion of what already belongs to God. Satan lost his place in the kingdom and refused to use his gift to serve God. Instead, he wanted to take the place of the One who created him. Everything Satan does is counterfeit, he tries to imitate Elohim, the Creator of heaven and earth. What a joke!

Well, it was obvious that this woman's life had been painful. She went through a great deal of loss. She had two children with two different fathers and was pregnant a third time by another man who had passed like the other two fathers. Without her saying a word, God revealed to Prophet Alph Lukau that this woman had three small incisions—one at the base of her neck, and inside both arms slightly below the forearm. When she was about seven years old, her aunt, (who was a witch and wizard) wanted someone to pass on this family altar to before dying. She took this child and initiated her by transferring ownership of this altar that she built. Unbeknownst to her this young girl became a witch and a wizard, and family heir to the altar. At night, this wizard's spirit would leave her body to fly around on a broom. When she became old enough to have relationships—the enemy began destroying her life.

She was involved in relationships with three men who loved her; however, each one died prematurely. Whenever this woman got angry, something terrible happened to the men she loved. When she had a disagreement with them, consequently, all [three] died in a car crash. She had no idea that an "evil" spirit was living inside her and causing pain. This broke my heart into pieces because at a tender age, this young child was burdened with her family's altar resulting in pain and devastation. Every man connected to her paid the price with their lives. She was not killing them naturally or intentionally—the evil spirit inside was. She took this ancestral altar involuntarily and was unaware of this evil pact with Satan. Being the firstborn in the family—she inherited it.

Another woman in attendance at that service was sought out by a family member to take her family altar. She was next in line to take over the family ancestral altar. But she said, no and the family member died without initiating her. One night while she was asleep, a familiar spirit appeared before her in a dream. This spirit looked like this same family member who died. It came to initiate this lady while she was sleeping. God showed this man of God this in the spirit, and she received her deliverance from this ancestral altar.

"Familiar spirits" disguise themselves as someone we know—alive or dead. Earlier, I talked about Satan being a counterfeit. He uses what we are familiar with in a feeble attempt to trick us. If we are not sensitive to the spirit, we will be deceived. The Bible says, *he even disguised himself as an angel of light* (2 Corinthians 11:14, ESV). We must be spiritually sensitive to know the difference and avoid being tricked.

Spiritual discernment comes when we spend time with God in the secret place. I had an encounter with a familiar spirit one night during my sleep. In a dream, a well-known prophet appeared before me. The prophet said, "Your husband and you are about to get a divorce." All of a sudden spiritual boldness arose within me in my dream, and I said, "Satan, the Lord rebukes you. The blood of

Jesus is against that, it is not going to happen!" The minute I released those words in my sleep, the prophet's face changed to someone I did not know.

Secondly, I received a call from one woman of God who shared a demonic encounter she had one night. She dreamed that her uncle—who she'd had a disagreement with while growing up—walked into her bedroom and raped her. When she woke up, she felt the residual pain of the rape. The face that the enemy used was her uncle's. Do know you why? The enemy thought if he showed this woman of God the face of her uncle defiling her, she would develop hatred toward him. However, it backfired. When this woman called me, the first thing she said was, "I know my uncle would *never* do something like this to me!"

I felt led to share these two examples; some of you reading this may not believe. You are probably saying, "No way is this real." Evil spirits are real! You may have been living here in the United States your entire life and never heard anything like this before, but it is true! I believe in America many people deal with some of the same demonic oppression. In most American churches, you really do not hear much about it, we hear a lot about generational curses or the spirit of death. Sometimes, we are not exposed to these demonic spirits and because we lack knowledge, a whole generation is wiped out.

One day, I was on Facebook and a famous gospel singer spoke out about losing eight members of his family in the last few years. Each year, a member of his family died. Then, if that was not enough, he was involved in a car accident that almost killed him. Right there, the Holy Spirit revealed to me when we have an assignment on our lives that *no devil in hell* can take us out before our time! This famous singer was supposed to be the ninth one, but God stopped it.

When I heard eight members of his family died, I was screaming to Facebook that this was the spirit of death, and someone in the family needed to break it! I prayed, *Lord, open his eyes to see this for what it is or send someone his way that knows the truth, so that another family member will not die before their time.* This is demonic. Either someone in the family opened a door, someone cast a spell on this family or Satan released this spirit of death in the lives of this family. Whatever the case may be, this is *not* God's will; this is a spirit of death that is wreaking havoc in this family.

In 2 Samuel 24:15, the Word of God says, the Lord released a pestilence that passed through killing 70,000 people. Remember this was in the old covenant; the way God's anger was poured out on the children of Israel, His wrath is not for us today. God's wrath was satisfied on Jesus; He was the propitiation (the provision given in our place) for our sins (Romans 3:25).

The Bible does say that *because of your callous stubbornness and your unrepentant heart, you are [deliberately] storing up wrath for yourself on the day of wrath when God's righteous judgement will be revealed...* (Romans 2:5, AMP). Therefore, God did not release the spirit of death into this family—Satan did. And here is why.

According to John 10:10, KJV Satan is *the thief whose purpose is to steal, kill and destroy: I am come that they might have life,(Greek word for life is zoe,* which means of its absolute fullest life) *and have it more abundantly.* I do believe at times people can open demonic doors for judgment, resulting in great devastation.

Still, I felt the pain of this servant of God. My heart was in pieces, the spirit of death was ripping this family apart. Sadly, no one in his family or anyone close to him saw this for what it was. The Bible says, *My people are destroyed for lack of knowledge...* (Hosea 4:6).

Most people may wonder where God is when all of this is happening. Some expect Him to come down off His throne to stop it. The truth is God has given us the authority to rule and subdue the world we live in. It is our responsibility to keep Satan under our feet; but if we are not spending time in the secret place, we are unable to see and hear. We accept what is happening as part of life and think that it is normal. God is not moving from His position; He has already given us the victory through Jesus (1 Corinthians 15:57). Therefore, it is up to us to decide whether we want to sit around and allow the enemy to wreak havoc in our world. The choice is ours—not God's!

This same spirit of death tried to show its ugly head in my family a few years ago. For three years in a row in May, a family member died. My cousin, who is a pastor and intercessor saw it for what it was. She prayed, fasted and the death cycle was broken. No one else in my family died in this cycle after she fasted and prayed!

I am not saying that *none* of my family members will *not* die and go home to be with the Lord—just not before their time. Someone in the family must commit themselves to fellowship so that their spiritual eyes can be cultivated to see in the spirit. Someone must be the spiritual watchman for their family. They must stand on the wall and say no to the appearance of evil. Can God use you to become the Nehemiah in your family? Will you be the one?

There was a well-known ritualist who dwelled in the same village where I grew up. Everyone from the surrounding villages and towns near and far came to see her. She claimed to have the remedy to cure all things. When someone needed answers, they would find their way to the village and the ritualist would tell them what they needed to know for a small price.

Over the years, she began training her firstborn daughter to take over her business to pass this altar to the next generation. This ritualist died years ago, and her daughter inherited her demonic altar. This business is still operating in the same small village to this day. This family altar was passed on voluntarily. Someone in this family needs to destroy this altar or it will go to the next generation.

The sad thing about these evil altars is that sometimes, they are kept secret in the family away from man. The good thing is nothing can be hidden from God. God is omniscient; He sees and knows everything. When I was a young girl, I would hide under my bed thinking God could not see me. Little did I know, God knows all things. He is present everywhere and He is all powerful.

In the eighth chapter of Ezekiel, the children of Israel thought they could hide their sins from God, but God revealed to the prophet Ezekiel what the Israelites were trying to keep secret in the temple. The Bible says, *Then the LORD said to me, "Son of man, look toward the north." So I looked, and there to the north, beside the entrance to the gate near the altar, stood the idol that had made the LORD so jealous* (Ezekiel 8:5, NLT). Why was the Lord jealous? The people had shifted their worship from Him to idols. *"Son of man," he said, "do you see what they are doing? Do you see the detestable sins the people of Israel are committing to drive me from the Temple? But come, and you will see even more detestable sins than these!" Then he brought me to the door of the Temple courtyard, where I could see a hole in the wall. He said to me, "Now, son of man, dig into the wall." So I dug into the wall and found a hidden doorway.*

"Go in," *he said,* *"and see the wicked and detestable sins they are committing in there!" So I went in and saw the walls covered with engravings of all kinds of crawling animals and detestable creatures. I also saw the various idols worshiped by the people of Israel* (Ezekiel 8:6-10, NLT).

The sin of the people was uncovered. Even more alarming Ezekiel 8:11 says, *Seventy leaders of Israel were standing there with Jaazaniah son of Shaphan in the center. Each of them held an incense burner, from which a cloud of incense rose above their heads.* The Israelites and elders in the temple had brought idolatry into the house of God. They created a secret room in the temple with a secret door to hide what they were doing; God revealed their sins to the prophet Ezekiel. But sin has consequences.

In the ninth chapter of Ezekiel, those who worshiped idols were killed. In chapter ten, the glory of the Lord left the temple because the people had contaminated the temple of God with idolatry. Some may think that they are hiding from God; He sees and knows all things. He is a God who reveals to redeem so we all can be free.

I have seen people who were into evil practices and right before they died, passed on their altars (equipment) used in the family home for rituals. In these families' homes, no one prospers. At times, no one gets married or has a fruitful life. There is no life around them; everything they touch turns to nothing because of these evil altars.

I have come to realize that the devil cannot bless us nor make us prosper. When an individual makes their decision to say *yes* to Satan, they are essentially signing their death certificate. If someone chooses to participate in evil deeds, their time clock begins to tick. Their life starts out looking good, although their destruction is right around the corner.

A couple of years ago, I was part of an international prayer group. We received a prayer request from one woman of God concerning a young boy who had been hit by a car. When we received the report, the young boy was lying in a hospital bed in a coma. We had no idea who he was, but we prayed and cried out to God for him like he was our very own son. I would pray so much each morning, I had to go immediately into the shower afterwards. I knew heaven was touched and our prayers were answered. After a while, we received the report that he had opened his eyes and was recovering. Then, his mother did something that changed the whole course of his recovery—she opened the door to evil. His mother went to a ritualist for a reading, seeking answers to what happened to her son. When she opened this door, the boy was dead within days.

I was sad and my heart was broken. I could not understand why for weeks, but I learned that darkness and light cannot mix!

The two are enemies. When we choose to access demonic altars and portals, we are literally choosing death over life. We must make the distinction between the two. We cannot have it both ways.

Many churchgoing believers still have open doors and access to evil. Sometimes, they get tired of waiting for God, thinking that He is moving too slowly. They cross over to witchcraft trying to get instant results. Remember the devil can never bless us. It is impossible for him to give us something that he does not possess. The devil can never release a blessing because he is cursed and as good as dead. His clock is ticking. When we open doors to him, death takes over like an uncontrolled wildfire.

I was honored to meet a sweet and precious woman of God through a family member. This woman of God is in heaven now, but when I saw her a couple months before she died, my spirit was alarmed. The minute I saw her, I observed the spirit of death all over her. Even though she was breathing, I saw no life in her. This woman was a believer who made a terrible mistake, changing the course of her life. She got involved with a man who openly admitted selling his soul to the devil. She lived with him and they became spiritually connected. This woman's physical health deteriorated rapidly. Before she died, she had so many complications, which included being legally blind. It was obvious that the enemy gained total access to her physical body.

When we open doors to the enemy, to me, it is like adding yeast into the right temperature with water and flour. Over time, it begins to take over the container as it gets bigger and bigger. My heart went out to this woman. I knew God had her in His arms, and where she is now, there is no more sickness or pain. What I learned from this is that we must be careful of who we choose to be in covenant connection with. It matters which altar we are connecting ourselves with; it makes a difference.

Some of you reading this book have not dealt with the evil covenant established by your ancestors or yourselves. You still have things around your home from earthly ancestors who opened the door to the enemy in their lives. These altars must be destroyed to move on to another level in God. These things have become your stumbling block, preventing you from moving forward. Evil altars built by your natural forefathers must be replaced to see a breakthrough or manifestation. The only way to establish a new covenant or altar in your life is to destroy the old ones.

Spiritual altars last forever if they are not destroyed. One Christian family had recently moved into a house they purchased. When they did their lives were in chaos. The previous homeowners had built an evil altar in one room of the house, where they communicated with evil spirits. The altar remained after the family moved. Altars will go from generation to generation if they are not destroyed. This family's livelihood was chaotic. Marriage began falling apart, children began acting up and their finances went dry. Once this family located the evil altar, they took anointed oil and poured it in the location where the evil altar was established. This is the only way peace was obtained when they destroyed this evil altar.

It is time to get rid of your voodoo dolls and free yourself from everything connecting you to anything demonic. The Word of God says, *All who fear the LORD will hate evil* (Proverbs 8:13, NLT). If we say we fear God, we will hate the sight of evil. When we are intimate with God, we get naked in His presence. We must begin to deal with what is hidden in the dark since God already knows. When we have an encounter with God like Gideon did, the Holy Spirit will bring what is hidden to the light, leaving us with a choice to make. Darkness cannot dwell in His presence. Before we can start something new, we must let go of the old.

Most people who get saved come out of evil covenants established by their ancestors or themselves. If they do, nothing moves. Their ways are blocked, and it seems like the enemy is wreaking havoc in their lives.

Apostle Guillermo Maldonado in Miami, Florida said his church was stagnant for many years. He went before God, and God told him, although the people in his church were saved, they needed deliverance. He obeyed God's instructions and the people received their deliverance. As a result, the church grew to thousands.

To move forward as a believer or a church community, we must break free from evil altars established either by us or family members. We break free by revisiting our past through the blood of Jesus. It is important when looking back on our past, we must first remember that it is covered under the blood. Most times, families do not want to deal with secret evil covenants. We would rather move on because we are saved and unfortunately there is some demonic oppression that is not dealt with.

God was about to do something new in the lives of Jacob and his family. He told Jacob to get ready to move to Bethel and settle there. He instructed Jacob when he got there to build an altar to Him. There was a problem: *Rachel stole her father's household idols and took them with her* (Genesis 31:19, NLT).

The first thing we must do to destroy evil covenants is to find someone bold enough to bring these covenants out, and it will not be a secret anymore. Satan knows he will not have a foothold over us anymore. Satan functions in darkness, and it is all over for him when he is exposed to light. This is why, when a young child gets raped, the rapist will say, "Don't tell anyone." Satan uses secrets to gain a foothold over his victim. A person receives their freedom when they open their mouth and tell someone.

While being on an international prayer line, one woman revealed that she was raped over forty years ago. She said she had never told a soul. After she was finished sharing her experience with the line, she said, "I feel like a whole load has been lifted off of me." Spiritually, this woman was held captive by Satan; finally, when talking about it, she received her freedom.

Pray and ask the Holy Spirit to lead you to the right person who will restore, love, and pray for you. Secondly, repentance and turning away from the way you used to live is important to your deliverance. Isaiah 61:10 (NKJV) says, *For He has clothed me with the garments of salvation, He has covered me with the robe of righteousness ...* (The Hebrew word for righteousness is *tsedaqah*, which means righteous act and righteous living).

Next, we must denounce and detach ourselves spiritually by our words. Heaven and earth are voice-activated, and we make a covenant with our words. The process works the same way to dismantle covenants. Moreover, if you know anything about sealing a covenant, it is usually sealed with blood. Do not worry, you have the power of Jesus Christ's perfect blood in your corner. All you have to do is release the blood over every evil agreement in the bloodline. Also, forgive yourself and never let the enemy place you in condemnation. You have already been set free.

Finally, the Bible says, *So they gave Jacob all their pagan idols and earrings, and he buried them under the great tree near Shechem*

(Genesis 35:4, NLT). Jacob told everyone in his household to get rid of all their pagan idols, to purify themselves and put on clean clothing. As instructed, Jacob built God a new altar and named it *El-Bethel*, which means "God of Bethel" (Genesis 35:7). We must get rid of our idols and anything associated with evil by burning them. If you are not comfortable with burning what you have, ask the Holy Spirit to show you a place to take your items. Gideon and Jacob both were moving into their new season and God was about to use them in a greater way; however, they could not move forward without first destroying the evil in their lives. Therefore, before you continue reading, stop and apply what we just spoke about to your life! Pray the following prayer:

Jesus, I believe you are the Son of God and you are the only way to God. Therefore, I confess all my sins and the sins of my ancestors that we have committed against you. I repent. Every evil door that was opened, by me or my ancestors, I close it now, in Jesus' name. I uproot and let go and break myself free from every evil altar, and I commit myself today to build up godly altars. I thank you, Lord; I believe, and I receive in Jesus' name. Amen!

For the remainder of this chapter, I will discuss how to build godly altars. Also, how I took my family's godly altar to another level. When we have a constant life of intimacy with God we build prayer altars that last a lifetime. What Jesus has done on the cross gives us access to this altar wherever we go. I am so grateful to God for my ancestors who built a godly altar of prayer with a righteous inheritance to take and pass on to my children and grandchildren.

When I think about intimacy, I cannot help thinking about my grandmother, Violda December. She was one of those *old* mothers of Zion who lived a life of intimacy with God. The fire of God burned in her and on her altar. People who came in her presence were greatly impacted. My grandmother left me a godly inheritance of intimacy. She knew God and He knew her, too. Not one day passed with her not being in the secret place of God. My mother migrated to the United States leaving my siblings and me in the care of my grandmother. I believe this was for a reason. God used this season to show me what true intimacy with Him looked like.

Every morning, I was awakened by the sound of my grandmother's fervent prayers. She was a strong, faithful woman of prayer. She understood the importance of prayer to live a victorious life. When she was faced with an obstacle, it was no challenge to her. She would turn her plate over and seek God with all her heart until she heard from heaven.

A long time ago, my dad went to live with a woman. And my grandmother disapproved because they were not married. For seven days she fasted and prayed. On day eight, my father walked out of the lady's house with his bags on his back. She knew how to use her spiritual altar to get results through her prayers. She was an example to me and many others who crossed her path. This great inheritance changed my life—I benefitted greatly through her prayers.

When I first received Jesus as my personal Savior, a burning desire arose in my heart for intimacy with God that did not go away. I attempted to wake up early in the morning to pray, which did not last long. I would lie in my bed and drift back to sleep. Naturally, I wanted that intimacy my grandma had for myself. God used her example. It was not just something she did on occasion. It was *daily* and intimacy was *who* she was. When something went wrong, she received answers and breakthrough from the Lord in each situation she faced, all because she had built an altar of God.

My grandmother lived in an underdeveloped country; her surroundings were not the determining factors for her character nor prayer life. She had a strong relationship with God. Whatever trial came her way, Jehovah Shammah was always there. Every morning my granny prayed and made you feel like part of her prayer. Her tongues of fire penetrated and would protrude through the walls. You knew heaven came to invade the earth. She was a demonstration of what it means to be intimate with God. She did not speak it, she lived it. God allowed me to glean from her life, and I had a hunger within me for intimacy. Even though God used my grandmother's example, He gave me a burning desire to be intimate with Him.

In 2012, I began to experience intimacy with God. The fervent longing for the Lord was fulfilled. I attended *Woman Thou Art Loosed,* and I believe this was a divine appointment with destiny. After returning home from Bishop T.D. Jakes' conference, he started a devotion entitled 52 Days of Pecking Orders. A prayer room was birthed with women who attended this event. Every morning for 52 days, women from all over the United States united to pray and seek the face of God. My life changed tremendously; intimacy was born. God used this prayer group to re-program us and from this encounter, I discovered little by little what God had deposited in me.

My appetite for the things of God increased. I craved more and felt uncomfortable where I was. I decided to start pursuing God's purpose for my life on a whole new level. My spirit was revived, and I felt brand new. A spiritual awakening was birthed within me and the people in my presence knew there was something different about me. Once awakened, I asked God for more of Him; I needed Him to tell me where I belonged, including my local church. After a while, I felt as though, I had outgrown it or did not belong there anymore.

Intimacy was already in me, and I learned over the years to take what my ancestor had left to create a much stronger fire. True intimacy builds an altar. It does not mean doing works, trying to pull God's hands to do something for us. Intimacy is about being led by the Holy Spirit into seeking the face of God with continual relationship or fellowship daily. It is communing with Him; we love being in His presence and cannot get enough. He draws us deeper and deeper when we spend quality time in His presence. The more He captures us—the more we want Him.

Chapter 2

The Holy Spirit Draws Believers Into Intimacy

*F*OR NO ONE CAN COME *to me unless the Father who sent me draws them to me, and at the last day I will raise them up* (John 6:44, NLT). None of us can be drawn to Jesus, unless the Father in heaven draws us. Again, we are not like the children of Israel who were far away from God. Believers are carriers of His presence through Jesus; we have been reconciled back to the Father. We cannot have intimacy with God in our flesh; it is not possible. Too often our flesh does not feel like communicating. Some days, we prefer to lie in bed. For the sake of our relationship, He pursues and helps us when we fall short.

Two years ago, I went to my brother's house in Mississippi for a family gathering. The four-bedroom house was packed. Every other room was occupied with pull-out beds. I was out of my comfort zone; intimacy was difficult. To me, intimacy does not always mean thirty minutes, I could not lie in the bed and pray, interrupting my husband's sleep along with everyone else in the house. Prayers were limited for the duration of my stay. My prayer altar was still in me. So, I even tried getting up, putting on clothes and walking around the neighborhood early in the morning; it just felt strange, and I missed my *intimate* fellowship with God.

I became too accustomed to sleep; when we finally came back home it continued. Thankfully, the Holy Spirit was there to help me when I needed Him. Later on, something supernatural took place. One morning I was sound asleep when all of a sudden, I heard the loudest bullhorn blowing in my ears. It was so loud I jumped out of my sleep. Then, I looked at my husband. He was knocked out! I thought to myself, *how come he is still sleeping after that loud bullhorn went off?* I realized it was supernatural after my husband did not move. If he had heard the bullhorn, he would have jumped out of his sleep, too. I immediately got out of the bed and said, "Yes, Holy Spirit, I hear you. I am coming now to get into Your presence." Thinking about this experience, I am even more thankful for the relationship with the Holy Spirit. I feel loved by Him.

When we do not feel His presence or feel like He is far away, we may not be spending enough time with Him. If we cannot hear His voice, it is probably due to distractions. The believer must be willing to pay the price to sit and wait (Hebrew Word for wait is *qavah*, which means to expect, whether in thought, in hope, to look for) for Him.

He wants us to meet Him. Hebrews 4:16 (NLT) says, *So let us come boldly to the throne of our gracious God. There we will receive his mercy, and we will find grace to help us when we need it most.* We can be overtaken by God's presence and release it wherever we go. Jesus made it possible for the believer to be a conduit of His presence.

At times, it is difficult to feel God's presence if distracted by the cares of this world that we deal with daily. I experience this frequently during a season of trial. The enemy tries to flood my mind to prevent me from being intimate with the Holy Spirit. While sensing His presence, my mind tends to wander; but I cast down those imaginations the enemy plants.

Fasting and praying are essential in the life of a believer. Killing the flesh, clearing the mind and spirit, allows the spirit to rule the body. I will discuss this in more detail later. The focus must be on God and not our problems. The believer will not enter into the secret place if our mind has no peace or clarity. We must purpose in our hearts to break free from the distractions to experience the tangible presence of God. If we are encountering God's presence daily, there will be His overflow from the inside out. We will be a light, and darkness cannot persist wherever we go. We will become an atmosphere shifter because we are in the light.

Pastor Benny Hinn, a well-known evangelist, lives a life of intimacy. He shared a testimony of one woman of God that he knew who was being tormented by demons. She decided to call him for prayer. The minute he answered the phone, the demons left the woman straightaway. The demons recognized the authority in his voice. He lives in the light and has the ability to shift the atmosphere and bring deliverance to anyone he comes in contact with.

I am reminded of the story in Luke 8:26-28 (NLT). When Jesus and his disciples arrived in the region of the Gerasenes, across the lake from Galilee it says, *As Jesus was climbing out of the boat, a man who was possessed by demons came out to meet him. As soon as he saw Jesus, he shrieked and fell down in front of him. Then he screamed, "Why are you interfering with me, Jesus, Son of the Most High God? Please, I beg you, don't torture me!* Obviously, these demons recognized the authority Jesus carried in the same way demons hear the voice of some believers. Jesus is the ultimate atmosphere shifter, and darkness did not stand a chance. *As Jesus is, so are we in this world* (1 John 4:17).

An accident had occurred after me and my husband left the grocery store. We stepped out of our truck and saw a frantic woman holding her baby. She hit a guy riding his bike and knocked him off. To the naked eye the guy seemed fine—clearly, he was in shock. He began going through the woman's truck.

Spiritual boldness came over me without a second thought. With authority I asked him, "Sir, what's the problem here?" The minute he heard my voice, he stopped and calmly sat down on the sidewalk. The atmosphere, once saturated with anger, fear, strife and danger, became calm and quiet. I was amazed by the instant turnaround.

One morning after prayer, I was traveling in a van with several believers. They asked me to pray, since I had been in God's presence earlier. Through this prayer, the glory of the Lord was released in the van so tangibly, every hair on my body stood at attention. Every single person there was affected. There was weeping, hands went up, and even the driver was touched by His presence! When the van reached its destination, everyone got out with praise on their lips. They were overwhelmed by the presence of God!

Another time, me and several women of God came together and went to a Virtuous Women's Conference in Orlando, Florida. The conference was great, despite the enemy's best attempt to steal the Word from us on our way back home. While we were headed to the Orlando airport, the subject of President Donald Trump arose. I really do not remember how the conversation started, it was clear that everyone had different views concerning the President, including the driver. Strife, tension, and contention invaded our midst; the atmosphere needed to be shifted.

I had spent three days in His presence and spiritual boldness arose. And once I opened my mouth to pray, the glory of God entered. During the prayer, my sister in the Lord who sat in the front seat had to remind the driver to keep his hands on the steering wheel. The Holy Spirit took over and I literally felt God's presence released. We arrived at the airport, and the driver was still overwhelmed by God's presence. We tried to tip him, and he said, "Mama, no tip; I've never heard anyone pray for me like that, thank you!" It was *not* me; I was only a vessel. He was affected through God's presence being released by prayers shifting the atmosphere. The Prince of Peace came into our midst and took over. The atmosphere did not stand a chance. Glory!

Every believer carries the presence of God being united with Christ. However, there is a difference between believers who sit in His presence constantly, and those who live without intimacy. Both believers have His presence; the believers who sit in intimacy daily have encounters in His presence. These believers live in the Holy of Holies walking in the His light. When the Lord's tangible presence emerges from the believer, He fills the room and it is difficult to shift from Him to something else.

One morning, not realizing that I had spent three to four hours in His presence, my location shifted. As I made my way up the steps, my feet started shaking, feeling the weight of His presence over me. Although I had not been drinking alcohol, I felt drunk. High off the Holy Spirit, His presence consumed me. Every fiber of my being could feel the presence of glory, I felt like I was floating in mid-air. A song came out of my mouth, and I began singing and worshipping God in the overflow. His presence is like tasting something sweet; the longer you have it in your mouth, the sweeter it gets!

We will never get tire of living in the secret place. We get to know Him more and more. Do not worry, the Holy Spirit keeps you on your toes. He spices up the relationship by pulling you deeper and deeper into intimacy. There are times when we are intimate with Him, we don't hear His voice. I have spoken to many believers about this, and they say it is not possible. However, I have experienced seasons where God is silent. In seasons like this, we must realize intimacy is never based on our feelings or what things look like. Intimacy is what we know about Him. God is there, although it feels like He is not. His Word says, *For in him we live and move and have our being …* (Acts 17:28). Hence, we are in Him, He is in us and nothing can separate us. He is quiet sometimes. For years, I researched Scripture to support reasons for God's silence, and I found three examples:

The first one that I found was when Saul walked in disobedience. The Bible says, Saul went to God after Samuel died, but God would not speak to him because he had disobeyed God's instruction. King Saul disguised himself and went to consult the medium of Endor (1 Samuel 28:7). He wanted instruction about what to do, so he went to the medium who brought up Samuel's spirit. What I have learned is, if there is unrepented sin in our hearts—although He still loves us—His voice can be silent.

The Word of God says, *If I had not confessed the sin in my heart, the Lord would not have listened* (Psalm 66:18, NLT). Saul sinned against God, and God rejected him. He could not get an answer.

The second example of God's silence is in the story of Hezekiah. The Bible says that Hezekiah was very wealthy and highly honored. But *God withdrew from Hezekiah in order to test him and to see what was really in his heart...* (2 Chronicles 32:31, NLT). Please understand, God will *not* leave us; I believe God's silence tests us to see what is really in our hearts. But do not lose faith. He will answer.

Lastly, in the story of Job, God was silent during Job's test. In the natural when taking a test, we are asked to turn off cell phones. Our seats are arranged so there is no direct contact with the person next to us. Before the test begins, we are instructed not to talk, and if we are caught talking or using our cell phones, failure is automatic. When we are going through a test, God is quiet, much like in the cases of Job and Hezekiah. God sees what is in us. Do not worry. *He will not allow the temptation to be more than you can stand ...* (1 Corinthians 10:13, NLT).

I must say that during the season of writing this book, I was being tested. Yes, God was speaking, and I heard His voice. What I was asking He was not speaking about. I realized that when the Holy Spirit is silent, we have the Word. Thank goodness any minute of the day, we can receive a Word to speak to every situation. The children of Israel did not have this luxury; thank God we do.

In the course of my testing season, I was so excited! I was on my way with friends to see a prophet of God. I was greatly expecting to hear a specific word from the Lord. As I sat in the revival meeting, my expectations were so high for God to use this man to speak a right-now word into my spirit. It did not happen as expected. I walked out of church with hurt feelings; I just knew it was not my time.

At this meeting, I realized a *real* prophet who hears from God cannot and will not speak what He did not say. If God is silent, there is nothing we can do—except wait on His timing. When service was over, one of my friends saw my disappointment. She pushed her way through and asked to see the prophet. She wanted to lift my spirit because she loves me, then suddenly, I was standing in front of the prophet. "What do you want God to do for you?" the prophet asked. When I told him, he laid his hands on me and prayed. Guess what? God did not speak. The prophet of God said,

"I see you writing," and I said, "Yes, I have written a few books." He released peace over me. That was it!

I was not really surprised. I am old enough in the Lord to know that I was going through a season of testing—and needed to exercise patience. If it is not the right season for God to release a specific word to us, it will be disappointing. If we try to push our way outside of God's timing. We will come up short.

Furthermore, as we read the story of Job, we can learn this same lesson. While Job was going through his ordeal, God did not speak for many chapters. Job and his friends did all the talking and they accused Job of doing something against God. They came up with their own conclusions why Job was going through his trouble. While Job was living in fear, he opened the door to the enemy. However, Job was being tested by God. The only voices Job heard were the voices of those around him. His foolish wife even told Job to curse God and die. Job was a faithful man and full of integrity. Instead of cursing God, he cursed the day when he was born.

In my season of testing, I was interrogated with questions like, "Did you check to make sure you are right with God? Maybe there is something you or your husband have done that opened doors." Also, it was implied that we were out of God's will—and we were told we were in the wrong church. We stood our ground in faith knowing God would deliver. I have learned that when going through a dry and difficult season we must: *Keep on asking, and we will receive what we are asking for. Keep on seeking, and we will find. Keep on knocking, and the door will be opened to us* (Matthew 7:7, NLT).

I believe God uses difficult season to propel us into maturity. What we know is that He will never abandon us and [we] must rest in His promises. What encourages me and renews my heart is pursuing Him through His Word. And even when it may seem like God is not there, He has promised: *He will never leave or forsake you* (Hebrew 13:5, NLT). In spite of what we think—God is there.

God is never in a hurry to do anything. There is a time and season for everything. In John 11, Jesus knew Lazarus was sick and needed His immediate attention. Jesus opted to stay where He was for two days (John 11:6). For His glory to be seen, Jesus took extra time in going to raise Lazarus. Mary and Martha told Jesus that if He had been there their brother would not have died. Jesus was not moved by their words. They had an emergency; Jesus still did not rush. We have deadlines and God is never moved by them. He is only moved by our faith in His Word!

Any believer can take five minutes from their day to pray and read a verse of Scripture. Real intimacy with God takes time. It is okay to start small, but do not linger there. The believer's intimacy should grow over time with the Holy Spirit's leading.

Sadly, many born-again believers do not experience this! Most do not understand the importance of spending time with the

Father. One day, a woman of God said to me, "It don't take all of that, Sister Maxine. You are doing too much!" Obviously, this believer had never tasted *true* intimacy. I believe if she had, her words would have been different. What she did not understand is it is the Holy Spirit who draws me closer to Him. Life gets busy and if I miss one day communicating with God, it is just like David said, my soul truly longs to be with Him (Psalm 84:2). My mind goes back to the last time we spent together, and then I become desperate for more of Him. Intimacy is not something we do religiously. We build it out of [our] love for God. If we are not intimately connected to Him, we will not be able to live life at our true potential. It is the believer's responsibility... *work out your own salvation with fear and trembling* (Philippians 2:12). What is amazing about having intimacy with God is; He draws us into fellowship. Our pastors, leaders or family members cannot answer this call for us; we must do this for ourselves. The benefit is what we do in secret, God will reward openly.

Have you ever wondered why the presence of God is more tangible in the life of *some* believers than others? I was scrolling through Facebook and saw a conference that was being held by a well-known preacher. He has two daughters. The oldest daughter is an anointed, well-known pastor, the youngest daughter is not as popular. At the conference, the younger one was asked to lead the prayer. Oh my! Her prayer shook 20,000 attendees as the world stood at attention. I felt goosebumps on my arms, legs and back as she prayed. My knees shook out of control—the Lord's presence was released from this woman of God.

People were commenting on social media, asking where she came from. She did not look like what came out of her. She was hiding, in the secret place, and I knew it. I was familiar with that place. God's fire burned an aroma from her life that shifted throughout the atmosphere, releasing the overflow. It was evident that she spent time with God the moment her mouth opened. His presence filled the room. I realize now that God's anointing and presence can be released by the most *unlikely* people.

There was a time when I believed I was counted out. Most of my childhood, I stuttered and could not hardly talk. No one understood what I was saying. In school, I was picked to be most unlikely to succeed. Thankfully, through God's grace, I was healed. It happened when I was watching a Christian television program. God sent a word of knowledge through a female servant, and miraculously I received healing. Thank you, Jesus! God had given me a yoke-breaking anointing—I discovered it through intimacy. The enemy tried to stop God's will from being fulfilled in my life. It did not work!

Here is some good news! Every believer has the power of God *within* them. Any believer can release God's presence and stand out from the crowd if they commit themselves to spending time with

Him. I absolutely love what Moses spoke to the Lord in Exodus 33:16 (NLT), He said, *How will anyone know that you look favorable on me—on me and your people—if you don't go with us? For your presence among us sets your people and me apart from all other people on the earth.* Glory! This is powerful! God's presence resting on the lives of believers sets us apart from others. God blesses and rewards faithfulness. The Bible says, *But without faith it is impossible to please him: for he that cometh to God must believe that he is, and that he is a rewarder of them that diligently seek him* (Hebrew 11:6).

Likewise, David said, *O God, you are my God; I earnestly search for you. My soul thirsts for you; my whole body longs for you in this parched and weary land where there is no water* (Psalm 63:1, NLT). David wrote this in his wilderness experience. He knew he could trust God's faithfulness to sustain him in a dry place. The secret to making it through difficult seasons is to spend time with God.

David sought God during the night [watch] and was blessed in return. *When I remember thee upon my bed, and meditate on thee in the night watches* (Psalm 63:6). Night watches were an important part of David's intimacy. He was an exceptional leader and warrior, God lovingly described David, as a man after His *own* heart. David loved and served God with his soul.

The night watch is the best time to pursue the Lord. Many times, when I needed answers concerning a [particular] matter it was during the fourth watch (between 3 a.m. and 6 a.m.), right before dawn, when I received my answers. The Word of God says, *He speaks in dreams, in visions of the night, when deep sleep falls on people as they lie in their beds. He whispers in their ears and terrifies them with warnings. He makes them turn from doing wrong; he keeps them from pride* (Job 33:15–17, NLT). God opens our ears to hear His voice throughout the night watch. He gives us warnings, brings correction, speaks, and gives us instruction.

There are four distinct night watches. I believe during the fourth watch the believer's spiritual ears are tuned into hearing God's voice the most. One word from the Lord will give us guaranteed results. If you are wondering, "Sister Maxine, are these watches of the night biblical?" The answer is *absolutely yes*.

In Genesis 32 Jacob wrestled with God during the fourth night watch. As a result, he received a blessing for not giving up. These watches are not only biblical, but according to the Smith Bible dictionary, the Jews, the Greeks, and the Romans divided the night into military watches instead of hours. The four watches coincided with a regular day in Jewish communities:

- The first night watch begins at 6 p.m., sundown on the Jewish calendar ending at 9 p.m. (Lamentations 2:19).
- The second night watch begins at 9 p.m., ending at midnight (Judges 7:19).

- The third night watch begins at midnight, ending at 3 a.m. (Exodus 14:24 and 1 Samuel 11:11).
- The fourth night watch begins at 3 a.m., ending at 6 a.m. (Matthew 14:25).

Intercessors are familiar with these watches. Their assignment is to keep watch. *Therefore keep watch because you do not know when the owner of the house will come back—whether in the evening, or at midnight, or when the roster crows, or at dawn* (Mark 13:35, NIV).

Witches and warlocks come out to perform rituals and sacrifices during the third watch. I heard an ex-witch (who is now a Christian) say at midnight she would "astral-project." This means the [evil] spirit leaves the body to roam around and carry out the assignment of Satan. Also, satanic worship takes place during the midnight hour.

On October 21, 2018, the news reported that after Justice Brett Kavanaugh was newly elected to the Supreme Court in Washington, D.C. witches tried to place a hex on him. It failed when intercessors showed up and stopped it. The reason for this example is to let you know that the hex took place after midnight. Seasoned intercessors in the faith are aware of this time. In this hour they do spiritual warfare to destroy the enemy's strongholds and plans—and receive lasting results.

My cousin, Pastor Paula Hazel, is one of God's faithful, [seasoned] intercessors. She has taught me so much. She lives in Guyana, South America, and she uses night watches to her advantage. She shared a testimony that changed my prayer life. She told me a gang of thieves held a village hostage in her community. Subsequently, people who came into that community were robbed at gunpoint. This continued until churches in the surrounding area decided to take action. They decided to do a drive-by.

A "drive-by" is when gang members literally drive by and shoot with the intention to harm or kill their targets. These believers were not shooting or killing people; they knew in order to see natural results, they had to deal with this spiritually. During the third watch, intercessors from that community drove their cars, traveling street to street binding the strong man of this village while praying. Something supernatural took place. Within days, everyone who was responsible for the robberies was caught and brought to justice. Thank you, Jesus!

The Bible says, *No man can enter into a strong man's house, and spoil his goods, except he will first bind the strong man; and then he will spoil his house* (Mark 3:27). What was the "strong man" in this community? It was the spirit of robbery and thievery. Do you know every city has a strong man? Some cities right here in America, such as Chicago, have a strong man or a territorial demon of murder. In my city in the state of Maryland, the territorial demons are religion and tradition. The reason all our communities have a strong man is because Satan's throne sits in the second heaven. From city to city, demons will hold the population hostage—unless believers stand in their God-given authority. Pastor Paula proved this to me when she bound the "strong man" in her community.

In the sixteenth chapter of Acts, it says, Paul and Silas began to sing praises to God at midnight (third watch) and a shift took place. The shaking from the earthquake caused the chains on Paul and Silas to fall off. Other prisoners' chains were broken, and their cell doors opened too.

Night watches bring stillness that creates intimate moments with God. Maximum results occur during this time. As a matter of truth, life changes for the better when God's voice is heard clearly by the believer. I have not only experienced this for myself, I have seen it in the lives of many believers.

I am the founder of the Meeting Place, a prayer ministry birthed out of intimacy with God. We help believers develop intimacy and grow in their relationships with the Father. I have seen drastic change repeatedly when God's people commit themselves to intimacy. Their lives become fruitful.

One woman came to our ministry diagnosed with internal bleeding. The doctors contemplated performing surgery on her. She had a timid personality and barely opened her mouth to talk.

She prayed quietly to herself and would only take part in corporate prayer. I saw God dramatically change this woman's life. Not only did He supernaturally stop the bleeding, this woman became spiritually bold and began to release a word of knowledge. She became a source of encouragement to people who came on the line.

Another woman told me she came to the ministry seeking prayer for her son, who was in desperate need of God. He could not hold a job, got involved with things outside of God's will, and refused to give his heart to the Lord. She even suspected that someone might have placed witchcraft on him due to his abnormal behavior.

One day turned into a year, and two and a half years later, she is still going strong. God brought her through so much. When her grandson was born, the umbilical cord had wrapped around his neck, causing him to lose a tremendous amount of blood to his brain. Eventually, he was placed on a respirator. The doctor said, he only had a 50/50 chance of living. We prayed and shook the heavens, believing God's report on his behalf, and God supernaturally turned his situation around. Today, he is alive and growing. Thank you, Jesus!

Every time I hear this woman speak, I praise God for changing her life. Her son, who was mentioned earlier, has a job and is moving forward with his life. Her testimony brings tears to my eyes. Surprisingly, he just walked into a local church and gave his heart to the Lord. Thank you, Jesus! In addition to God blessing her son, she received the Holy Spirit with the evidence of speaking in tongues—right in the Meeting Place. God also gave me the opportunity to lead her daughter to Christ right inside the comfort of her home.

This same godly woman who came to the Meeting Place to obtain prayer for her son has evolved. Her life is changed forever by the presence of the Lord. When no one else wants to pray, she faithfully shows up and moves forward!

Spending time with God pays off. Consistency with faith is crucial to manifestation and fruitfulness. The same thing (and greater) can happen to you—if you are willing to pay the price to sit in God's presence daily. God will surprise you! The believer must respond to the drawing of the Holy Spirit. If He wakes you up in the middle of the night, it is not to go on social media. God is waking *you* up to come before Him. Do not ignore His prompting; your life will *never* be the same again.

CHAPTER 3

THE SECRET PLACE REVEALED

*A*ND ADAM KNEW (INTIMACY) EVE *his wife; and she conceived, and bare Cain, and said, I have gotten a man from the LORD* (Genesis 4:1). When I think about intimacy, I cannot help thinking about the earthly relationship between husband and wife—God's original intent for mankind. Intimacy can also be between animals or any human being such as friends or family. According to the Merriam-Webster dictionary, intimacy is the state of being intimate. It is to have a close familiarity, friendship, and closeness. Furthermore, when I think about intimacy my relationship with my husband comes to mind.

We know each other in ways no one on earth does. We are acquainted and bonded together deeply. The intimacy we share is not only for nighttime, it encompasses the day. We are intimate in our conversations, touch, and the way we look at each other. All day long, hearing his voice still makes me feel chills down my body.

When holding me in his long arms, he makes me feel safe and protected from harm. When we are apart for a long time, I feel like something is missing in my life and I cannot wait to be with him. In fact, God is the reason why we share this intimacy. He is the ultimate lover. He is love, and because of our encounter with His love, we are able to express our love and share intimacy together.

Intimacy is not only for mankind to experience with each other, God desires to have intimacy with His bride, the church. He created man to have fellowship with Him. Adam lost his dominion on the earth when he sinned, forfeiting his fellowship with God. However, thank God for Jesus, who became the last Adam who restored man back to the place where he belongs (1 Corinthians 15:45). Through Jesus, mankind returned to God's original intent—to a place of fellowship, safety, and security.

Every believer who desires fellowship with God can find Him in the secret place. The Bible says, *He who dwells* (Hebrew word for dwell is *yashab*, which means to sit down, to remain, to be set, stay) *in the secret place* (Hebrew word for secret place is *cether*, which means covering, shelter or hiding place) *of the Most High Shall abide under the shadow of the Almighty* (Psalm 91:1, NKJV). Therefore the secret place is a place of covering; it is a shelter and a hiding place where God is.

Our heavenly Father *hides His beloved ones in the sheltered, secret place before His face,* (Psalm 31:20, TPT). We are safe from those who conspire against us being in His presence. Every believer has access to the secret place—the Holy of Holies—through the blood of Jesus. It is a dwelling place where God lives. Nothing is lacking in the secret place. All needs and desires are met, and dreams fulfilled. In the secret place, there is healing, fruitfulness, and abundance. Nothing is missing or deficient; it is a place of total wholeness.

In the old covenant, the Israelites did not experience this; the spirit of God did not live on the inside of them. Only once a year, the children of Israel came from near and far to give their offerings to the Lord to atone for their sins. The Ark of the Testimony in Exodus 25 was foreshadowing what was to come. It was a temporary dwelling place where God would come down and fellowship with man. The word "tabernacle" in Hebrew is *mishkan*, which means dwelling place. Thus, a tabernacle is a place where God's spirit dwells.

The only person allowed to enter the tabernacle was the high priest. Once a year, he went into the Holy of Holies to offer sacrifices on the Day of Atonement for his sins—and the sins of the people. However, the children of Israel were not even allowed in the outer court. They brought their offerings and stood outside the gate.

Thank God for Jesus our High Priest. He made it possible for us to have a far better covenant. Jesus became the perfect sacrifice and gave us direct access to God (Hebrews 8:6-7). Today, instead of walking miles and miles to atone for our sins, Jesus has already taken away our past, present and future sins, once and for all.

Believers live in the reality of the actual intent God had for the tabernacle. The minute an individual says yes to Jesus as their personal Savior, their body becomes the tabernacle or dwelling place of God. *Under the old covenant, the priest stands and ministers before the altar day after day, offering the same sacrifices again and again, which can never take away sins. But our High Priest offered himself to God as a single sacrifice for sins, good for all time. Then he sat down in the place of honor at God's right hand* (Hebrews 10:11—12, NLT). No longer are we separated from God's presence. Born-again believers are given access, not only through the gate, but also into the Holy of Holies. Jesus said, *I am the Gateway. To enter through me is to experience life, freedom, and satisfaction* (John 10:9, TPT). The believer finds life behind the veil, which no longer separates God and His people.

The place where God's presence dwells is no longer a building; He dwells in us. The Bible says, *Don't you realize that together you have become God's inner sanctuary and that the Spirit of God makes his permanent home in you? Now if someone desecrates God's inner sanctuary, God will desecrate him, for God's inner sanctuary is holy, and that is exactly who you are* (1 Corinthians 3:16–17, TPT). God dwells on the inside of the believer; the presence of God comes from the inside out. The only sacrifice needed is time spent in His presence.

Dwelling in the secret place introduces you to experience the supernatural power of God. He becomes your covering, shelter, hiding place, and in Him you find protection.

When we are intimate with God, *in the time of trouble he shall hide us in his pavilion: in the secret of his tabernacle shall he hide us; he shall set us up on a rock* (Psalm 27:5). There were many storms I had to face. Without a shadow of doubt, I knew that because I was in the secret place with God, He protected me and gave me the strength to overcome.

For example, one day there was a knock at my door. A man presented me with a summons to appear in court. When I opened the letter, I felt *total* peace. I was being sued by a creditor for money I owed them. I was surprised by my response. Because I start my day in His presence, there was total peace. God had me covered under His wings. Family members could not understand it, but I was stress free.

I had no idea where the money was coming from; I knew it was already done. The first thing that came out of my mouth was, "Baby, we are not going to set one foot into the court because I believe it's paid in full." This was faith speaking. We did not have any money saved at that time. I knew we served a God *who was able to do exceeding abundantly above all we can ask or think …*

(Ephesians 3:20). I went about my days and weeks with the total peace of God.

A couple weeks later, the money we owed was paid in full. We did not borrow money from any financial institution or person. What we declared by faith came to pass. My husband and I did not set a foot in the courtroom. God used someone that we least expected to take care of the amount that was owed. Thank you, Jesus!

We walked through this situation—and many others like this—with the peace of God pouring out of me. I can boldly say, it was because we dwell daily in the secret place with God. He gave us the strength to walk through the storms of life without fear.

I have experienced God's delivering power and His peace to walk through trials. As a result, we came out on top. In Psalm 23:4 (KJV), David said, *Yea, though I walk through the valley of the shadow of death, I will fear no evil: for thou art with me; thy rod and thy staff they comfort me.* God was there with David to comfort and guide him every step of the way.

Just like David, we too, must not fear evil—this is the only way God will hide, comfort, and protect us. His peace will sustain us through any storm of life. We will receive His strength to walk through life's difficulties.

Chapter 4

Waiting for the Lord

WAITING FOR THE LORD IS oftentimes overlooked during intimacy; we do not have time to wait for the Lord. Our full schedules take priority over waiting on the Lord or spending time in His presence. One thing I have learned from my relationship is during intimacy, He is *never* in a hurry. It is possible to sit down and be in a position for the Lord and not experience the fullness of His presence. Why? The price must be paid with our time when we wait for Him. I am not saying God is hard to find. We are His temple and we can access Him anywhere. Waiting is an important part of being intimate with Him.

The Word of God says clearly, *But those who wait for the LORD [who expect, look for, and hope in Him] Will gain new strength and renew their power; they will lift up their wings [and rise up close to God] like eagles [rising toward the sun]; they will run and not become weary, they will walk and not grow tired* (Isaiah 40:31, AMP). In exchange for waiting, God will renew our strength and we become full of His power. He raises us up to bring us closer. We will not get weary. Believers are rewarded with His presence waiting in expectation. The more we sit in expectation for the Lord in the secret place, the closer He brings us to Him. Then, we will experience His goodness.

The reason this chapter is entitled *Waiting for the Lord* is not that I am trying to say the Lord's presence is far away from us; I am saying that He is in us. We are triune beings, and God's presence is in the Holy of Holies (spirit). It takes time to break loose of the flesh and soul (mind, will and emotions), get rid of life's distractions, and tap into the spirit. The Bible says *that no one can stand before him and boast about anything* (1 Corinthians 1:29, ERV), meaning our flesh must die before we can encounter God's tangible presence. When we practice waiting, then layer by layer our flesh will fall off. Every believer can have a sense of His presence. They must break away from the body and soul to enter the Holy of Holies.

Looking at a man from the outside in, we see his body, his soul, and his spirit, which is the dwelling place of God. A body filled with distractions and worldly cares prevents us from tapping into the dwelling place of God, which is our spirit. God's presence is attracted to stillness. His Word says, *be still,* (Hebrew word for still is *raphah*, which means to relax, to let go, to be quiet) *and know* (Hebrew word for "know" is *yada*, which means to know by experience, be acquainted with) *that I am God* (Psalm 46:10). Believers get to know God when they relax, let go, are quiet and wait for His presence. Real intimacy is not for the faint of heart or for someone too busy. It is for whomever will make God their number one priority.

The reason some of us cannot experience God's tangible presence is that we are either too tired or busy. In Acts 1:4–5 (NLT), Jesus told His disciples, *Do not leave Jerusalem until the Father sends you the gift he promised, as I told you before. John baptized with water, but in just a few days you will be baptized with the Holy Spirit.* There is no way I am saying these verses are a formula for receiving the gift of the Holy Spirit or experiencing Him. Any born-again believer can receive His gift with the evidence of speaking in tongues by faith at any given time. The disciples were about to receive power and they had to wait for a specific moment for it to arrive.

Waiting for the Lord's presence is not a formula. It is a position of expectation and faith to experience God's goodness. The Holy Spirit answers those who are desperate and hungry. If we are desperate enough, we are not moved by time or our surroundings.

When a church service's atmosphere is saturated with desperation, God *never* disappoints His people. He shows up powerfully—and He is experienced throughout the service. God shows up when His people are desperately crying out; and there has to be *unity* among the believers. *And when the day of Pentecost was fully come, they were all with one accord in one place. And suddenly there came a sound from heaven as of a rushing mighty wind, and it filled all the house where they were sitting* (Acts 2:1–2, NKJV). Unity is strength—not only naturally, but also spiritually.

The minute we sit and desperately cry out, "Lord, I long to be in your presence" and wait, He will forcefully engulf our entire being and take over the room. Expectation is an important part of intimacy and should not be skipped. If we wait, we will experience and enjoy His supernatural presence.

A few years ago, I desperately needed a financial miracle. I came across an old song by Dr. Juanita Bynum entitled, *I Don't Mind Waiting*. Without realizing how powerful waiting was, I began to work a miracle. I started singing and the Lord's presence filled the room. I totally let go of my need and began to worship, telling Him, "I don't mind waiting on you, Lord." Worship lasted about an hour, and later that day I received an unexpected check for almost $5,000 in the mail. Glory to God!

Waiting gives us rest. When we rest, God's favor appears. God will not disappoint us when we wait for Him. Waiting allows us to abandon our own agenda to surrender to His agenda. We can relax with full assurance that God will show up. If we are not willing to pay the price by waiting for the Lord, we will not experience His presence tangibly. After we have tapped into the Holy of Holies, we encounter the voice of the Holy Spirit. Even when we pray, we should be still and wait in expectation for Him. David knew how to wait for the Lord. He said *I wait quietly before God, for my victory comes from him* (Psalm 62:1, NLT). Will you practice waiting for the Lord your God today?

Chapter 5

Prayer: The Most Important Conversation of the Day

A COUPLE OF YEARS AGO, my cousins Pastor Paula and Sister Yvonne Waldron came to my house. As they began to pray, I could not help asking how they prayed like that. They moved from one thing to another without a single thought. I told them I do not pray like that. Sometimes, I do not even know what to say to God. The Scripture they shared with me was the start of my prayer life.

The Holy Spirit helps us in our weakness. For example, we don't know what God wants us to pray for. But the Holy Spirit prays for us with groanings that cannot be expressed in words. And the Father who knows all hearts knows what the Spirit is saying, for the Spirit pleads for us believers in harmony with God's own will (Romans 8:26–27, NLT). In other words, I must depend on the Holy Spirit to pray *through* me. This explains why during prayer, I did not know what to say because I was depending on myself.

The Holy Spirit guides us through our daily prayers. We depend on Him, not our flesh to tell us how to pray, what to pray and how long. If He wakes us at midnight leading us into prayer until 5 a.m., then follow His lead. Most non-praying believers think that everyone starts praying on level ten. In Luke 11:1, the disciples of Jesus asked Him to teach them how to pray. Obviously, Jesus prayed often and gave His disciples *The Lord's Prayer* as the model.

The first step of prayer is the believer must be available to be used by God. Even if the believer starts out speaking a few words with no idea what to say, consistency is the key to progress. We must be willing to begin a lifestyle of prayer. Prayer is essential in the secret place; it is how we communicate with God. Live a life of prayer and God will use you!

One night, I was dead asleep. After midnight, I heard an *urgent* whisper in my ears. "Get up, it's time to pray!" the voice said. There was urgency in this voice, I jumped out of my sleep. My heart was beating so fast, it felt like it was about to pop out of my chest. I started praying in tongues. Soon after, I called my family to make sure everyone was okay.

Then, the voice of the Holy Spirit spoke; it was Him who woke me up. He needed access on the earth through my prayer.

When I looked at my phone, I saw a verse reassuring me, all was well; there was no need to be afraid.

God needs us to intervene on earth. He gains access by impressing the heart of an intercessor or any believer to pray. Ezekiel 22:30–31 (AMP) says, *I searched for a man among them who would build up the wall and stand in the gap before Me for [the sake of] the land, that I would not destroy it, but I found no one[not even one]. Therefore, I have poured out My indignation on them; I have consumed them with the fire of My wrath; I have repaid their way [by bringing it] upon their own heads," says the Lord GOD.* Sadly, as we see in these verses, God sought for someone to stand in the gap on behalf of the land and He found no one. As a result, judgment was pronounced. If someone on earth does not pray, then God's will cannot be done on this earth as it in heaven.

In some churches, prayer meetings receive the least attendance. Not every believer is called to be an intercessor or prayer warrior. Some believers lack understanding of how essential prayer is, so they do not pray at all! Without prayer, we cannot have intimacy. Every time a prayer meeting is called, you can literally count the number of believers who show up to pray. Jesus said, … *My house shall be called the house of prayer* (Matthew 21:13). If Jesus called His church the house of prayer, that indicates it is essential to the body. A church that does not pray is weak, *powerless* and serves as a bad demonstration of Jesus. A *prayer-less* believer is a *powerless* believer.

We are not receiving the desired results in our lives due to prayerlessness. We are not praying God's will for what is already in heaven to come to earth. Thus, we fall short in giving Him access into our earthly situation. Instead, we make excuses by saying God is allowing that situation to persist in our lives. I am not saying that immediate manifestation occurs when we pray, or that God will not allow us to walk through some trials. Some believers will say God allowed them to get sick to teach them a lesson, *this is a lie from hell.* We must realize that God is *not* the one always holding up our breakthrough—or His answer to our prayers. God has seasons for everything (Ecclesiastes 3:1); however, there are times the enemy will withhold answered prayers in our lives, and we may blame God.

Apostle Paul wrote to the church in 1 Thessalonians 2:17–18 (NLT) saying, *Dear brothers and sisters, after we were separated from you for a little while (though our hearts never left you), we tried very hard to come back because of our intense longing to see you again. We wanted very much to come to you, and I, Paul, tried again and again, but Satan prevented us.* They wanted to go back to the church; Satan hindered them from doing what they had purposed in their hearts. Also, in Daniel 10, when Daniel was praying and fasting for twenty-one days—the prince of Persia held up his answer. The angel appeared before Daniel and said, *Since the first day you began to pray for understanding and humble yourself before God, your request has been heard in heaven* … (Daniel 10:12, NLT). Michael the archangel came, fought, broke through the blockage the prince of Persia had set up and Daniel received the answer to his prayers.

The body of Christ must be careful not to use the message of grace as an excuse *not* to have a prayer life. I thank God for grace—without it, *every believer* would be lost. Grace is not an excuse or license to be lazy and not have regular communication with God. If God is responsible for allowing everything bad in our lives, that would leave the enemy nothing to do with trying to prevent us from receiving answered prayers, then there is a problem.

If God allows everything bad to happen in our lives, what can we say about the woman who had five miscarriages? Every time God opened her womb she conceived and ended up losing the baby. As a result, she goes deeper and deeper into depression. Do you think God did this on purpose to test her patience? *Of course not! It is a big lie!* What kind of God would open the woman's womb, change His mind, and allow the enemy to take her baby each time? He would be a giver who gave and decided to take it back. *The blessing of the Lord makes a person rich, and he adds no sorrow with it* (Proverbs 10:22, NLT). This is not the God we serve; this is the enemy's doing.

The enemy does not want believers to be blessed, he tries to destroy what God has given us. But, if believers live a life of prayer, their spiritual discernment will develop and they will know the difference. When we are faced with life situations; we must ask ourselves the questions: *Is this from God? Did I open this door in my life or is it something the devil has set up as a barricade in my life?* If it is the enemy, the Lord revealed to me in a dream how to blow up the barricade the enemy set up.

One night in a dream, I saw myself on a journey. I was walking on a long path that led me through the woods and over a bridge. I came to some train tracks that appeared to be old and black. I was about to place my feet on the tracks and noticed some of the wood was missing. The Holy Spirit instructed me to lay flat on my stomach with both hands on the tracks. Suddenly, the missing wood came supernaturally back into place. I got up and walked to the other side. I came to a wall that had climbing rings that allowed me to climb up the wall. When I made it to the top, there was a small square space; I needed to crawl through to get to the other side. As I began crawling through the small space, a demon came out of nowhere and stopped my flow. All of a sudden, a wooden door came down in front of the demon shutting off the path in front of me.

Then, I heard the voice of the Lord speaking to me. "Do you know how to unblock the barricade?" the Lord asked. I said, "No, how?" "Build me an altar. When you build me an altar, I will provide the fire and the barricade will blow up." I woke up out of my sleep. Wow! Do you have a blockage? Are you stagnant in your business, ministry, finances, relationships or anywhere else in your life? If so, build the Lord an altar of prayer. As we learned earlier, an altar is a place of intimacy and a gateway to heaven. When we have a daily prayer life through intimacy with God, He will provide the fire to blow up the enemy's roadblocks that hinder you from moving forward.

This dream was prophetic. The journey symbolized life. Sometimes the enemy's barricades are set up to prevent us from receiving answers to prayers or moving forward as seen in Daniel 10. The Holy Spirit revealed to us an important key to dealing with barricades that come across our path.

Prayer must be done in faith. Faith is the vehicle that moves the things already given to the believer in the spiritual, into the natural. Prayer opens heavens and closes the portals of hell in our lives. When we are available to the Holy Spirit, He will use us to intercede for others.

One Sunday in church, I received a text from my sister, informing me that my son's father went to see his probation officer and an Immigration and Customs Enforcement (ICE) officer arrested him. It made my mind unsettled. So, I gathered my belongings and went looking for my husband; he was serving outside in the parking lot. Fear came into my heart and I began shaking in disbelief. After finding him, my husband held me in his arms and said, "Maxine, he will not be deported." When my husband released those words, fear disappeared. I responded, "Baby, you are right; he will not be deported." From that day on, I knew I needed to be strong and that prayer was critical to see his freedom.

I called some people I knew who could pray and believe God with me. I asked them to join me in prayer. However, as I reached out, some asked, "Maxine, isn't he the one who caused you so much pain in the past?" I responded, "Yes." I knew what they were thinking, *Why would you want to waste time praying for someone who caused you so much pain?* He reaped what he sowed. However, I was not interested in what they thought. I was only interested in doing my Father's business. When it comes down to prayer, my husband and I do not discriminate. To us, prayer, love, compassion, grace, and mercy are free. We were given these things freely, so it was an honor to extend it to someone else.

Furthermore, my son's father is part of our family. Our son would have been devastated if deportation were final. We needed God to intervene. I could not wait to get into the prayer room the following morning, so the warriors could join me. Saints of God, this was not easy. In the beginning, the report was not in his favor. Things looked so dark that the enemy began showing me him being deported. At one point, the judge began to speed up the case. According to the lawyer, it was so that he could be deported.

During that time, I woke up between the hours of 3 a.m. and 6 a.m. to lay flat on my belly and cry out for mercy on his behalf. I asked the Lord to touch his life and to give him an encounter that would change his life. "Lord, visit him, and let him be a living witness for you," I prayed. Then, slowly things began to shift. The days seemed long when he went to court, and we thought it was the day. Things started happening and I knew that in spite of what it looked like, God was still on the throne. Three times in a row, the lawyer was supposed to show up in court and fell gravely ill. Constant prayer on my altar was essential.

I knew we needed a Word to stand on. I thank God for my spiritual mom, Apostle Cynthia Brazelton, who I believe is an apostle of the Word of God. Months earlier, she gave the church Job 22:30 (AMP), which says, *He will even rescue the one [for whom you intercede] who is not innocent; And he will be rescued through the cleanness of your hands.* Along with this Scripture, we stood on Colossians 2:14, (NLT). We prayed, "God, thank you for canceling the record of the charges against him and for taking it away by nailing it to cross." Then, we thanked God for my son's father's freedom; whom the Son sets free is free indeed (John 8:36).

This process took about eight months. In September of 2018, he walked out of that place free. Thank you, Jesus! I was overwhelmed when I found out that he was baptized in the facility where he was kept for eight months. He was the one who God used to preach to others who were being held by ICE. I asked God to change his life, and I did not know how God was going to do it. He did! God uses our situations for His glory! All the glory belongs to God! The heavens were opened, and the gates of hell were closed!

Again, I believe prayer is mandatory for the believer and it is *not* optional. It does not matter how things may look to the naked eye. God needs a faithful vessel to bridge the gap to bring His purpose from heaven to earth. *Are you the one?*

A believer does not get to pick and choose whether they want to engage in prayer or not. The believer *must* pray. A prayer-less life signifies a life of defeat. It is the responsibility of the believer to cultivate or build an altar of prayer.

When Jesus came to the earth, He had a healthy prayer life. In Luke 6:12–13, Jesus went up to the mountain to pray, and He prayed all night because He had an important decision to make. At daybreak, Jesus called all His disciples together and chose twelve to be apostles. Everywhere He went He would speak one or two words and people's lives were instantly changed. He lived a life of prayer.

In Genesis 1:26–27, God made man in his own image and likeness. God gave them dominion to rule the earth. In other words, God gave man jurisdiction on earth. He gave man the official power to make legal decisions, to enforce His judgment on the earth. God will *never* break jurisdiction, so that is why without man's prayer, which gives Him access into our earthly situation, He *will not* intervene without an invitation. The Bible says, *The heavens belong to the LORD, but he has given the earth to all humanity* (Psalm 115:16, NLT).

Believers are responsible for getting into position to rule the earth they live in. If the believer does not rule the world, then Satan (the god of this world) will rule in their place. As soon as God sees one of His children in danger, He impresses on the heart of another available believer to pray. When believers pray, access is granted, and God intervenes in their situations.

One rainy day in December 2016, while at home preparing for Christmas. I decided to bake a cake and forgot that I needed eggs. I asked my son to go to Walmart to buy some. Fifteen minutes later, I received a call from him. When I picked up the phone, I could tell that something bad happened; I heard distress in his voice. He said, "Mommy, I was in an accident," and he began gasping for air. My heart skipped a beat. I began praying in the Holy Spirit—I needed God to go where my son was to bring comfort and peace.

I went to the accident scene and saw my son sitting in the car on the side of the road. The rear end was damaged beyond what my eyes could see. I got into the car and asked him if he called the ambulance. He gasped for air as he tried to answer my question.

"The ambulance came, and the police took a statement. The person who I hit, left because there was nothing wrong with him nor his vehicle, not even a scratch," my son replied. I knew it had to be some supernatural intervention because the insurance company deemed my car as *totaled*; they gave us the money and sold the parts. Although my car was not salvageable, thank God, my son was fine and had no injuries—not even a scratch.

As I was sharing this testimony of God's hands on my son's life, my friend said, "Oh Jesus, the Holy Spirit had impressed it on my heart during the same time of the accident to pray for you and your family. The Holy Spirit did not reveal what was wrong, so I just began speaking in tongues while I was in the store." Wow! I was so grateful to God that she followed the leading of the Holy Spirit and prayed. Thank you, Jesus!

God needs access in the earth. I believe with all my heart that we must pray aggressively. The Word says, *The kingdom of God suffereth violence, and the violent take it by force* (Matthew 11:12). I am a living witness of what violent, constant prayer can do. I have seen tremendous results. My daughter made eight attempts to pass *one* test. Each year, she would get frustrated and give up after each attempt. My husband and I prayed, encouraging her to push forward. She would take the test and it would come back with the same results. I got tired of seeing her in distress and decided that enough was enough. It was time to get violent!

Jude 1:3 encourages us to earnestly contend for our faith. We fasted, spoke the Word, cried out, gave a seed, and used our faith. Still, nothing manifested. It is not that these spiritual tools do not place believers into position to receive, the enemy had a blockage set up, so nothing changed!

When my daughter went to take the test in 2018, I told the devil that he would lose! I declared this was the year of harvest and no more delay! As she took the test, my husband and I agreed to pray in the Holy Spirit. The prayer warrior rose within me, and the enemy had no choice but to give it up. I made a commitment to intercede the entire duration of her test or until I felt the shift in the spirit. I prayed so much, sweat ran down my face, but I kept praying.

During the prayer, I had a vision. I saw my daughter in the room with her head bowed at the screen. I released an angelic host to touch the screen, then something supernatural took place. When I felt the shift in the spirit, I began laughing and singing in the spirit. I danced before the Lord; I knew victory would manifest that day. My daughter passed the test that very day!

But, she did not even take her money to pay for the exam because of previous disappointments. She had already decided in her heart, she was not going to pass. *But thanks be to God, who always leads us in triumph in Christ* (2 Corinthians 2:14, AMP).

I knew the angelic hosts did what I assigned them to do when she said, "Mommy, I was in shock because the answers were just coming to me on the computer. I kept checking my answers right. I knew it was a miracle." This miracle took a long time to manifest but I am a living witness that prayer works. Although my daughter had lost hope during this process, our God is faithful. When I saw the pain, shame and feeling of inadequacy my daughter was enduring, I would cry out, "Lord, my daughter needs you! Help my daughter, Jesus; when will it be her turn?" During that time, I learned that it does not really matter how long the wait; victory is *sure*. Once we stay consistent in prayer and faith, God will manifest His glory on our behalf!

The Word of God says, ... *that men ought always to pray, and not to faint* (Luke 18:1). Regardless of what is happening in our lives, we must dedicate our hearts and minds to prayer. We may not have a chance to pray every day for an hour; I do not think it is possible. But if we dedicate five minutes of prayer while driving, we are still communicating with God. We must practice His presence daily. We can make our steering wheel an altar—but do not stop there. In the same way, my friend was tuned into the Holy Spirit in the store, He will bring a person before us to intercede for. Most times, I am led to pray in the Holy Spirit, considering I have no idea what they are going through.

Prayer is great medicine for the soul. His Word washes the soul; prayer keeps us connected to the source of life. If we do not have a connection to God, I cannot imagine what man would do without fellowship with the Holy Spirit.

I had the opportunity to take a course in Comparison Religions. It was disturbing to learn that most religions pray to a dead god. They do not have a relationship with the gods they are praying to. I cannot imagine praying to a god who does not hear me, cannot talk back to me, cannot answer my prayers and cannot even fellowship with me.

It is important to know that prayer is *not* a monologue; it is a dialogue. Believers speak to God and allow Him to speak back. This part of prayer should not be skipped. Pastor Gloria Copeland once said, "You haven't finished praying until you listen." If we pray for three hours in the secret place and say "amen" without listening for the Holy Spirit's response, our prayers will not be fruitful.

Not every believer has trained themselves to hear the voice of God in complete silence. Some believers train themselves to hear God's voice during prayer. In fact, some believers can be praying loudly, yet have their spiritual ears tuned into the voice of the Holy Spirit simultaneously. What is vital is listening for the voice of the

Holy Spirit and not *only* speaking to Him. We should give Him a chance to speak. In the secret place believers not only develop our spiritual hearing, we develop a relationship with our heavenly Father.

Have you ever had a conversation with someone who talked from beginning to end, nonstop? They dominated the entire conversation and did not give you a chance to respond. This is a *one-sided conversation.* The same applies to someone praying who does not listen for the Holy Spirit. These prayers are also one-sided and fruitless. I call them fruitless because one word from the Holy Spirit has the ability to change our lives. If we are doing all the talking and not listening to the Holy Spirit, then instruction and answers to our prayers are missed. Therefore, we must make room during or after prayer to listen and learn the voice of the Holy Spirit. He wants to tell us what we need to know.

James 5:16 (TPT) says, *Confess and acknowledge how you have offended one another and then pray for one another to be instantly healed, for tremendous power is released through the passionate, heartfelt prayer of a godly believer!* When I think about family members and how God used me and my husband's passionate, heartfelt prayers to intercede on their behalf, my heart is forever grateful.

One of my nephews recently graduated from Marine boot camp. I know without a doubt that he made it because of God's grace and the prayer of the righteous. Although my nephew grew up with family, the spirit of rejection and anger plagued his life. He was not doing well and constantly got into trouble at school in New York. My husband and I agreed to let him live with us and give him a fresh start. Every day, we received emails or phone calls from teachers concerning his bad behavior. One day, he cursed a teacher out so bad, they suspended him from school. After arriving home from school, we disciplined him. We would have done the same for our children, if they needed it. The following day, he did not return home from school. We received a phone call telling us to come to the school. When we got there, the school had called social services and initiated an investigation.

Oh my! My heart was broken. I knew we did nothing wrong. When they called my own children to question them, it shocked me to my core! We had nothing to hide, I just felt violated. No wrongdoing was found during the investigation. My nephew's behavior worsened and we decided to send him back to New York with his father. He started smoking weed excessively. The enemy would tell me that he would "end up in jail." I began using the Word of God to tear down those imaginations the enemy had shown me concerning my nephew.

The Word of God is the incorruptible seed that lives and abides forever (1 Peter 1:23). Our family held on to Isaiah 54:13. We would say, "(His name) is *taught of the Lord and great is his peace."* Every time my mom would call for prayer for my nephew—it did not matter what was happening—we declared the Word. Although in the natural, it seemed like it was not working, we continued to declare the Word over his life.

In January 2016, my church, Victory Christian Ministries International went on a corporate fast. My pastor, Cynthia Brazelton, encouraged us to include family members in the fast. I called my mom and sister in New York and encouraged them to join me in fasting and praying for a week, believing God for the shift in my nephew's life. On the third day of the fast, as we finished praying and declaring Isaiah 54:13, something supernatural took place. After we hung up the phone, my nephew called my sister and said, "Auntie, I am done with this. I can't do this anymore; I am going to stop smoking weed. I am done!" The very next day, my nephew rededicated his life to God. Hallelujah!

I wish I could tell you that he was done indefinitely—that would not be the truth. Over the next few weeks, my nephew showed signs of slipping back into his old lifestyle. I thank God, for my time with the Holy Spirit in the secret place. He has given me spiritual discernment. We must be alert and keep watch so … *that Satan will not outsmart us* (2 Corinthians 2:11, NLT). We must get familiar with his evil schemes and prepare for when he comes at us, we can boldly tell him, "No devil! Not today or ever."

Satan needs our words to agree with what he is showing us. This is the only way he will gain access to us. One day during her sermon, Pastor Cynthia said that sometimes, we will be tested with our testimony; and that is exactly what happened.

The enemy tried his best to steal my nephew's testimony by giving him the desire to go back to those things God had already delivered him from. The more evil reports would come in, the more I would say by faith, "Satan, the Lord rebukes you. He is already delivered. I see what you are trying to do, but he is taught of the Lord and great is his peace and I release *peace* over him now!" Discernment is heightened sitting in the secret place and we can see the enemy's tricks a mile away. Consequently, I was not moved by how things appeared to be. I know what the Lord has already done. Thanks to God, for giving us the victory in Christ Jesus.

All the calls completely stopped. He is serving our country in the military. God brought him through and will take him into a successful future. All the Glory belongs to our God!

The secret place of God is a valuable place for the believer. But, if we are not careful, we will present the same needs to Him over and over. I have learned that if we allow the Holy Spirit to rule our prayer life, He will lead us through prayer. He is the king of our hearts. It is never about us and all about Him, we must give Him total access to us, so He can pray through us.

Praying in the spirit is supernatural and powerful! I believe it is essential for Christian living. If we pray in the spirit daily, we can become spiritual giants. I know a man of God who before he went out to preach, he spent weeks in advance preparing to minister by praying in the Holy Spirit. He spent no less than six to seven hours a day speaking in the spirit. When the time came for him to minister, his anointed voice sent demons running. Not only in the service, it extended to the people next door, even they received deliverance. His sermons were full of revelation of the Word. This godly man was a spiritual giant.

If someone desires to become stronger in prayer, they must dedicate themselves to consistent prayer. The above example displays a man of God, who wanted to get spiritually stronger and committed himself to praying in the spirit. Clearly, he learned from Apostle Paul who said, *I thank God that I speak in tongues more than all of you* (1 Corinthians 14:18, NIV). Apparently, Apostle Paul tapped into the importance of praying in the Holy Spirit.

We can conclude that Apostle Paul spent quality time praying in the spirit. We should pray in tongues daily to … *build ourselves up in our most holy faith* (Jude 1:20). I have come across many believers who were taught to wait for a [certain] feeling before praying in the spirit. And if the feeling did not come for two years, then they would not speak in tongues for two years. But, Ephesians 6:18, (ERV) tells us to *Pray in the Spirit at all times.*

I love praying in the spirit and I love the fact that ... *people won't be able to understand you* (1 Corinthians 14:2, NLT). For me this is priceless; Satan does not understand what we are saying and cannot hinder our prayers. As believers, we must pray in the spirit—hence, the devil cannot understand what we are saying.

When praying in the spirit, God releases the believer's destiny and purpose in the heavens specifically for us. I heard several believers say they had a desire for open doors to preach. Once they committed to praying in the spirit daily, doors started opening. They began to receive invitations to minister the gospel worldwide. Praying in the spirit brings whatever is in the spirit to the natural world around us.

Some mornings, after the alarm clock sounds, waking me up for prayer, my body and emotions start talking. "Stay in bed. You just went to bed. Your weekend was full, just stay in the bed." Soon after I drag myself out and slowly walk toward the couch. The first thing I say is, "Good morning, Holy Spirit." Even before we get out of bed, we should acknowledge the Holy Spirit. He is our ... *Helper, (Comforter, Advocate, Intercessor—Counselor, Strengthener and Standby)...* (John 14:16, AMP). The Holy Spirit is our closest friend.

Sadly, I believe sometimes He can be overlooked or not even acknowledged for who He really is to us. When I need supernatural strength, I am always amazed that it comes all over me from praying in the Holy Spirit. Believers baptized in the Spirit can receive supernatural strength. We build ourselves up just by praying in the Holy Spirit. Our spirit will stir up quickly; we must pray from our bellies and let it come through our mouths, *…out of your belly will flow rivers of living water* (John 7:38). Therefore, whenever we pray in the Spirit from our bellies, we feel a stirring very quickly. Praying in tongues is one of the most powerful and rewarding things believers can do. When we have no idea what to do in the natural, the Holy Spirit has the answer. We must tap into the spirit to get God's will.

My son walked down the stairs one morning and said, he was going to buy a new car. He was eighteen and wanted to purchase it without any guidance from me or my husband. For a moment I thought, *He is eighteen, the car dealers are going to eat him alive.* Instead of allowing fear to creep in, we just let him go. The minute he walked out the door, my husband and me held hands and prayed in the Holy Spirit for about ten to fifteen minutes. We could not physically go with him, but the Holy Spirit could.

With no idea as to what God's will was concerning this matter, we agreed to receive it in Jesus' name. Something supernatural transpired; a few hours later my son came back with his brand-new red car. My heart skipped a beat. But, I knew the Holy Spirit was at the dealership with him. Our main concerns were his monthly payments and interest rate. I asked him about it, he received an interest rate at one percent (1%). He said the salesman told him that he *never* seen someone that young receive such a low rate. I had never heard that before either. Have you? My son paid off this car in a little over three years! I thank God for my spiritual mom, Apostle Cynthia teaching the importance of praying in the spirit. It works!

We pray and miss at times when it is against God's will. Kenneth E. Hagin once said, "Faith begins where the will of God is known." If we do not know His will concerning a particular situation, it benefits the believer to lean and depend on the Holy Spirit. Religion tells us to wait for a feeling to pray in the Holy Spirit. I can tell you from experience, that without praying in the Holy Spirit, I would not know what to do.

The Word of God says, *When someone speaks in tongues, no one understands a word he says, because he's not speaking to people, but to God—he is speaking intimate mysteries in the Spirit. The one who speaks in tongues advances his own spiritual progress, while the one who prophesies builds up the church* (1 Corinthians 14:2–4, TPT). In other words tongues edify the believer. The word "edify" in Greek is *oikodomeō*, which means to build up, restore, and repair and grow in wisdom. Hence, praying in the spirit builds up and restores those who are broken.

Once Sunday before church service started, a woman came and sat right next to me. When I greeted and hugged her, she broke down in tears. I held her tightly and heard the Holy Spirit say, "Tell her there is purpose in your pain!" When I released those words into her ears, she fell out! Oh man, I did not expect her to fall out. I was led to kneel over her and begin to pray in the spirit. I had no idea how to minister to her, I just knew the Holy Spirit already had the answers. All I needed to do was obey.

While speaking in tongues over her, I had a vision. As I spoke in the Spirit with my eyes closed, I saw a man carrying her in his arms. Then, I heard the Holy Spirit say, "Tell her I am there with her in the middle of what she is going through. I am carrying her right through it." When I told her what the Holy Spirit gave to me, she held me and cried. "Before coming to church, I prayed that the Holy Spirit would give a word especially for me and He did," she said. "I desperately needed to hear that!" Thank you, Jesus!

We desperately need the Holy Spirit to heal, restore and build up the broken. We cannot do this on our own. When we speak in tongues, the spirit of God works through us, yoke-destroying power is released through our mouth.

Here is another example of how powerful praying in the spirit is. My mother-in-law was visiting and while eating dinner, I believe that I experienced a demonic attack. Every part of my head started hurting to the point it felt like I was about to lose my mind. My eyes hurt so badly, I could barely open them. Then, I heard the enemy say, "You are about to have a brain aneurysm, and you are about to die. What are you going to do?" I could not think straight or even open my mouth, it was extremely painful. Words were difficult to formulate—speaking to the enemy was not in my mind.

Nevertheless, I thank God for my mother-in-law, who knew how to pray and tap into the Holy Spirit. Holding my head with both hands, she began praying in tongues. After a while, I joined in. I held her and we prayed in the spirit. At first speaking in tongues was painful, but I was not paying attention to the pain. After praying for about fifteen minutes, my headache completely disappeared. I praised God like I had lost my mind. He is a healer. For the first time, I recognized how *powerful* praying in the spirit was.

My oldest brother turned forty-seven years old in 2019. I cannot recall one season in his life when he was free from migraines. Growing up, I witnessed the excruciating pain my brother endured. As an adult, his pain worsened, making it difficult for him to work and participate in daily activities. His battle with migraines debilitated him for weeks with no relief in sight. The same year, after consulting his doctor who ran many exams, they found nothing. He was told several times that there was nothing they could do to get rid of the migraines. The best they could do was give him the usual painkillers that became ineffective.

I knew my brother had reached his breaking point. As his sister, watching the pain he suffered over the years was difficult. I'd had enough of what the enemy was doing to my brother; I called to offer him prayer. He had been lying in bed with a migraine for days. Before opening my mouth, I felt prompted by the Holy Spirit to pray in the spirit. I explained to my brother that I would be praying in the spirit. I told him not to worry about what I would be saying. I just wanted him to close his eyes, lift his hands and receive.

I told him the power of God was about to fall on him. And the migraine from hell that he had battled since childhood was leaving him, in the name of Jesus. I began praying in the spirit over my brother. My mother who was in the room with me, also prayed in tongues. The prayer lasted for about eight minutes. When I felt the release in the spirit, speaking in English I commanded that devil to turn him loose and let him go. I commanded him to be healed in the name of Jesus! My brother did not receive instant results, though the next day when he woke up, the migraines that plagued his entire life had completely vanished. Thank you, Jesus!

Prayer should not be taken lightly; it brings life to the believer. Nothing happens in the kingdom without prayer. When revival is birthed forth, please understand that it did not just happen. God used a group of people or someone to sow in the ground or geographical areas with prayer and fasting to bring revival into the earth. Some believers are sowers, and some believers are reapers.

God is the One bringing the harvest of souls. He is the Lord of the harvest.

Anna was a prophetess who ... *told everyone in Jerusalem that the anticipated Messiah had come* (Luke 2:36–37, TPT). The Bible says, she worshiped God in the temple day and night fasting and praying. God used her as a spiritual midwife to bring forth what was spoken. Midwives or intercessors must stand in the gap praying for God's will on the earth. In the first chapter of Exodus when Moses was born, there were two midwives present to give aid in the birthing process. The Hebrew word for "midwives" is *yalad*, which means "bring forth, bear or travail." Anna was a spiritual midwife God used to bring forth what was already fulfilled in heaven to the earth. These midwives always knew His secrets; they are seated in the secret place of God with their spiritual ears open. When God needs access on the earth, a midwife or an intercessor must be in position to pray His will. Things may not be happening in your life if you are not praying!

This explains why some believers have no idea what God is doing with certain matters. They live their lives from earth to heaven, and not heaven to earth. When we live our lives from the [third] heaven to earth, we know the will of God. We are not moved by what is going on in the earth. *The secret of the LORD is with them that fear him; and he will shew them his covenant* (Psalm 25:14). Once believers live in the secret place with God, the Holy

Spirit will reveal His secrets for them to bring forth His will in the earth.

I attended the Virtuous Women Conference for my birthday on October 12, 2017. I woke up early for prayer and I said, "Okay Father, today is my birthday and I am asking you to give me something special." Later that evening when I returned to my room, the Holy Spirit told me to go across the hall over to my friend Margaret's room to pray together and shift the conference to another level. I told Margaret that we did not come all this way to have church as usual.

We sang and ushered in the presence of God. Next, we began to speak out His will in tongues, then in English. We prayed and prayed until the shift was felt, and then stopped. Thank God for doing it. The glory of God filled that room and it was powerful! When we finished praising and giving thanks, Margaret who is from Uganda said in English, "Lord, change our names today, give us a new name the same way you changed Jacob's name." This was the heart of God for the conference that night, but (we) midwives needed to take time to pray God's will on the earth. Margaret prayed in the spirit for the will of God. The Holy Spirit gave her the interpretation to speak the prayer in English without her even realizing it.

When we left the room for the conference something supernatural happened. The speaker that night went to the microphone and prayed this, "Lord, we didn't come all this way to have church as usual; give us an encounter that will change our lives." It was as though she had listened to our prayers. I almost fell out of the chair in astonishment. When she introduced the message title, I almost ran out of the room. It was about God changing our names and giving us new ones. Wow! God is perfect! He gave me something special for my birthday; He gave me a new name.

Here are more demonstrations of God's will on the earth as it is in heaven through prayer. One of my Facebook friends logged on to my prayer livestream. After I saw him logged on, the Holy Spirit led me to pray for him. I prayed in the Holy Spirit then said in English, "Lord, I called his name; give him an encounter with you that will change his life forever." I released myself and prayed in the Holy Spirit again. I thanked God for what he had done.

About one to two weeks later, something else supernatural happened that blew my mind. I found out my Facebook friend who I prayed for, drove from Queens to Brooklyn and had no idea how he got there. All he remembered was, waking up in the Intensive Care Unit (ICU) with a blood sugar level of 1500. The prayers of the righteous helped, he made it out of ICU. When I finally talked to him, he shared his encounter with God. He recalled seeing and experiencing heaven while asleep in ICU. God took him on a trip to heaven, changing his entire life. Grateful to be alive, he rededicated himself to serving the Lord totally. Wow, I was overwhelmed to be used by God that way.

Another morning during prayer, the Holy Spirit prayed through me in the same manner for children who were kidnapped, abused and held against their will. Out loud I prayed, "Lord, make a way for them to escape through a door or window in Jesus' name." About forty-eight hours later, while on the computer I saw breaking news. Thirteen children living in California had been terribly abused. Starved, beaten, and chained by their parents in prison-like conditions.

These children were severely malnourished, never attended school and never received medical care. But God! The supernatural part about this miracle was one of the children escaped through a window and ran for help. What I discovered from this encounter with God—there is no distance in prayer. God needs someone who is available to be used. Are you the one?

Remember, God answers our prayers, but at times if we are not in the spirit, we miss God. We see this in Acts 12. The believers interceded on behalf of Peter, and God granted their request. However, they did not believe their prayer was answered that quickly. So when we pray, let us not be like those disciples who were not expecting God to answer. On our prayer altars, we must look for God to show up at *any* given time.

Chapter 6

Fasting Is Intimacy

AS MENTIONED EARLIER, the Father draws us by His spirit and gives us the desire to seek Him. It is the same way He draws believers deeper by His spirit into a period of *fasting*.

Fasting is not a practice, believers do religiously; its main purpose is intimacy. The Holy Spirit divinely leads the believer into fasting. Fasting is a physical action producing a supernatural result. With fasting the believer goes deeper by positioning their ears to hear and receive what God has already given us before this world's foundation. Fasting is a command by God, not an option. It can be done either individually or corporately. Jesus fasted for forty days and forty nights. The Bible also highlights others who fasted alone and corporately.

Joel 2:15–17 says, *Blow the trumpet in Zion, sanctify a fast, call a solemn assembly: Gather the people, sanctify the congregation, assemble the elders, gather the children, and those that suck the breasts:*

let the bridegroom go forth of his chamber, and the bride out of her closet. Let the priests, the ministers of the LORD, weep between the porch and the altar, and let them say, Spare thy people, O LORD, and give not thine heritage to reproach, that the heathen should rule over them: wherefore should they say among the people, Where is their God? No one is excused from this corporate fast, not even the children. God commanded His people to consecrate themselves before Him with fasting.

Every January, most churches worldwide start the year communing with God. They gather corporately to fast and pray. One January while sitting in church, an elder announced that the corporate fast would begin the following day. Oh my! The mood of the people went from ten to zero. Immediately after the announcement was over, there was complete silence. I thought to myself, *we are not really interested in it.* We fail to understand fasting brings us into a deeper place with God.

Whenever fasting is mentioned, we often think about the food aspect. Although we are abstaining from it, believers should *think* intimacy. Intimacy is the real reason we fast and pray; and in exchange, we are spiritually empowered. When the believer fasts, the spiritual man gets stronger and the flesh gets weakened. Whenever I think of intimacy with God, I am not sad at all. In fact, I am excited to get into His presence. Some believers only fast once a year; I am not here to criticize anyone. The main purpose of this chapter is to give believers a better understanding of fasting's importance.

Here are some truths. The reason the congregation's mood changed when the elder mentioned fasting is the flesh cries out, "No!" The thought of leaving macaroni and cheese, chicken and banana pudding for a period seems unbearable. Clearly, the flesh is in control—not the spirit. Remember, man is a three-fold being—spirit, soul, and body—according to 1 Thessalonians 5:23. If the flesh is always in control, then we are on the path of destruction. There is no good thing in our flesh. In the spirit, there is eternal and abundant life. The flesh says, "I want it. Give it to me. I want it now!" Most things our flesh craves come from the world we live in. *For the world offers only a craving for physical pleasure, a craving for everything we see, and pride in our achievements and possessions. These are not from the Father, but are from this world* (1 John 2:16, NLT).

Fasting breaks our cravings for things of the world. Even though we live in the body, we are more spirit than flesh. The Bible tells us to, *let the Holy Spirit guide your lives. Then you won't be doing what your sinful nature craves. The sinful nature wants to do evil* (feed the flesh), *which is just the opposite of what the Spirit wants. And the Spirit gives us desires that are the opposite of what the sinful nature desires. These two forces are constantly fighting each other, so you are not free to carry out your good intentions* (Galatians

5:16–17, NLT). This is the reason why when a fast is called, the whole church goes silent. The spirit man wants to obey—the flesh wants to fight and stay in control.

Apostle Paul tells us how to deal with the flesh. We must discipline our bodies like an athlete, training it to do what it should (1 Corinthians 9:27, NLT). Believers must train their bodies to do the will of the Father and obey the spirit. Believers cannot walk with God at greater levels unless our spirits rule over our lives. It is important to put the body under subjection to the spirit. Do you know we can talk to our bodies? We are the masters of our flesh, and it must obey! I did not realize the control we have until the Lord used my husband to illustrate what it really means to discipline or take control of my body.

I went away to a women's conference one October. When my husband picked me up from the airport, my body knew I was headed home. Out of nowhere, I felt the urgency to use the bathroom. My stomach felt like it was about to flush itself out, whether I liked it or not.

"Baby, I have to use the bathroom and I don't think I will make it home," I told my husband with fear. I felt a push coming. Speaking was not a good idea. I was trying to concentrate while my husband drove. After two minutes passed, "Baby, it's coming!" I yelled. "Speak to your bowels and tell it to go back up, in the name of Jesus," my husband instructed. When he first said it, I thought this man was losing it. "Go ahead and try it," he encouraged. "It's going to work." Being obedient I said, "Bowels, I command you in the name of Jesus to go up now, in Jesus' name!" What happened next was shocking. My bowel movement was literally on its way out. When I spoke to my bowels—without delay—I literally felt it go back up. The urgency to use the bathroom went away. We made it home and when I went to the bathroom, there was no delay.

I heard a man of God say, unexpectedly he felt like throwing up. He said it was coming whether he wanted it or not. He thought waste should not be coming out of his mouth and it is going the wrong way. With boldness, he said, "Stop! Go back down and come out the right way!" Suddenly, what was about to come through his mouth went in the opposite direction. Why did this happen? He had control over his own body.

I just received this in my spirit as I was writing. If the doctor said there is sickness in your body, keep in mind that your body belongs to you! Open your mouth now, and renounce that sickness! Call it by name, tell it to leave your body now. In the name of Jesus! Speak to that part of your body where sickness is—and command it to be healed! Believe and receive what you just declared. Glory!

Prior to this, I had not realized the control that I had over my own body. I get to decide what goes in, rule my body and tell it what to do. We can discipline our bodies and tell them what to do or what not to do. I learned during a fast, I can tell it, "No, you will not be eating for twenty-one days, so hunger pain be silent now. I am in control!"

Who is Lord in your life? Is it Elohim or your belly? Philippians 3:19 (NLT) says, *Their god is their appetite, they brag about shameful things, and they think only about this life here on earth.* The believer controlled by flesh has their mind on earthly things that will not last forever but will fade away. Food is not our God; it is what we need to survive. The Word of God tells us ... *Man shall not live by bread alone, but by every word that proceedeth out of the mouth of God* (Matthew 4:4). If we can control our bellies, we will subdue our flesh. For a period, the believer can live on the Word of God. It is spiritual food! While fasting the believer must place natural food aside and digest spiritual food.

Fasting positions the heavenly transfer of things God has already given to us through Christ Jesus to the natural world. Our fasting must be purposeful. Before the fast begins the believer must declare it out of the mouth. Words are powerful. If we do not proclaim the fast with our mouths, it is unlikely we will finish. Declaring the purpose of our fast is also important. If the fast is called without establishing a clear purpose, when it is over—there will be no spiritual results. If believers decide to fast for intimacy with God, or to hear His instruction for the family, it should be verbally established.

Throughout the Word of God, when God's people called a fast, they had purpose behind it. Esther, for example, called a three-day corporate fast after hearing about Haman's plan to destroy the Jews. The children of Israel fasted, and abstained from food and water. They believed God for favor as Esther prepared to go before the king unannounced. God rewarded Esther as she received spiritual boldness and favor in return for risking her life to see the king (Esther 4–5).

In 2 Chronicles 20, the armies from Edom declared war on Jehoshaphat and the children of Judah. The Bible says Jehoshaphat was afraid of the news, and he called a corporate fast in Judah to seek God's instruction and guidance. Jehoshaphat and the rest of Judah turned their faces to the wall, prayed and cried out to the Lord for help. God heard their prayer and saw their sacrifice. The Lord sent a word to Jehoshaphat and gave him divine instruction. In the end, the Lord defeated the enemies of Judah. They were in the position for divine intervention. This congregation fasted and prayed with a purpose; God answered and delivered His people.

In the first chapter of Nehemiah, we find another great example of fasting with purpose. When Nehemiah heard that the wall of Jerusalem was torn down and the gates had been destroyed by fire, he mourned for many days, fasting and praying before the

God of heaven (Nehemiah 1:4, NKJV). Nehemiah needed favor with the king, as he began his journey to rebuild the walls and gates of Jerusalem. The Bible says in the end, the king granted all the requests of Nehemiah. The hand of the Lord was on his life, and he positioned himself with fasting and praying before he took his request to the king.

The following are two powerful, life-changing testimonies of fasting and praying with *purpose* I heard while livestreaming at AMI in Johannesburg, South Africa.

The church was on a seven-day corporate fast during the month of July. When the fast was over, the prophet of God called out a man from thousands of people who attended the service. The man had been through several dead-end relationships and desired to find a wife. He had no idea that he was coming to church to meet his wife that day. What happened next was beyond supernatural.

"God is giving you, your wife today," the prophet told the man. Then, he told the man to stay seated and pray. The prophet also told him that he was going to find her in the crowd. The man of God went into the crowd and God divinely led him to locate a woman who would eventually become his "future" wife. Nevertheless, the next part is what I really want to get to.

The woman who was picked had fasted and prayed with the church for seven days. Coincidentally, she cried out to God for a husband. Every day during prayer, she said, "God, I am getting old. I need my husband." She took this petition to God daily and when the fast was over, He answered the woman's request. What she did in secret, He rewarded her openly. After fasting and praying—*with purpose*—she was connected with her future husband that God manifested in her life.

One pastor was being severely tormented by the enemy through a member of the leadership committee at the church that he was pastoring. When he took on his new role as pastor, an elder (a seasoned member) in the church leadership began to persecute him. She had great influence on other leaders within their local body who sided with her. The pastor tried everything to settle this matter, to no avail. Things worsened over time and his life became a living nightmare. The man of God decided to go before God for a short period of time concerning this dilemma. The pastor met God at the same place daily, crying out for the Lord's help. This lasted for about a month. One day after pouring out to God, he fell asleep and had a vision. Someone appeared to him and said, "Wipe away your tears, the time is up. I will deal with (Elder's name)."

Not understanding the vision, the pastor called the committee's chairman and asked him to explain the vision. While on the phone, he heard an explosion coming from inside of his church. He ran outside his office and observed the wall in the middle of the room had [suddenly] collapsed. The elder who the enemy used to make the pastor's life miserable was passing by the wall when it collapsed—crushing her to death. When they uncovered the body, the elder was found dead with her Bible in her hands.

When I heard this testimony, I could not speak for several minutes; I was speechless! This pastor had a problem, set his face to the wall with purpose, then petitioned God for help. And He came through. I am sure this man of God was not praying for this particular outcome. When we allow the enemy to use us, doors are opened for judgment. *For the time is come that judgment must begin at the house of God: and if it first begin at us, what shall the end be of them that obey not the gospel of God?* (1 Peter 4:17).

God's grace is extended to everyone daily. *The Lord is not late with his promise to return, as some measure lateness. But rather, his "delay" simply reveals his loving patience toward you, because he does not want any to perish but all to come to repentance* (2 Peter 3:9, TPT). Sadly, everyone does not choose to take His free gift of repentance. As a result, this opened doors for destruction.

David fasted and prayed, hoping for his first child with Bathsheba to live. Even though he sacrificed himself through fasting, his son did not live (2 Samuel, 12:15–23). I love Psalm 135:6 (ESV), which says, *Whatever the LORD pleases, he does, in heaven and on earth, in the seas and all the deeps.* God is still sovereign!

These two stories of the pastor and David teach us that when we fast, pray and sacrifice ourselves before God, the outcome does not always turn out in our favor or how we would prefer. During these times, we must *trust* God. We may not understand what He allows, however we must remember that He will bring us to our destination.

Fasting does not move God; it moves us closer to God for supernatural results. The believer must know before proclaiming a fast that: *Every spiritual blessing in the heavenly realm has already been lavished upon us as a love gift from our wonderful heavenly Father...* according to Ephesians 1:3, (TPT). Therefore, we are *not* fasting to try to create something. We are fully loaded with all spiritual benefits in heavenly places. We are healed, rich, delivered, forgiven and totally free because we accepted Jesus as Lord.

My grandmother made many supernatural transfers through fasting and praying. I shared this testimony in my book, *Krazy Faith*. My grandmother knew God. A while back my sister was having chest pains and my grandmother took her to the doctor. The doctor told her that my sister needed open-heart surgery. My grandmother decided that was not going to happen, so she called a fast.

She turned her plate over for seven days and called on Jesus. Seven days expired and she took my sister back to the doctor. My sister was examined again, and nothing was found. God had supernaturally mended her. They decided that my sister did not need the surgery after all. Fasting produces supernatural results.

Real fasting will quiet our hearts and souls. It postures us to hear from God and receive answers to our prayers. During one season of my life, before my son finished high school, things became difficult in my home. The next thing I knew, my son moved out, and he went to live with his girlfriend and her family. I was upset about the move—it was not something we practiced in my family. I needed God's intervention, so I went on a seven-day fast. I declared with my mouth that if my grandmother got results during her fasts, so can I.

I did an all-liquid fast for seven days. I would lay on my son's bed each day and call on Jesus. After the seventh day, I felt breakthrough. I checked the mail and received a letter from the post office saying that my son had changed his address. I knew God heard my prayers and saw my sacrifices. The enemy was trying to tell me otherwise. "All that fasting was for nothing, you wasted your time," the enemy said. I got violent and said, "Satan, the Lord rebukes you! If my grandmother could pray and get results, so can I." About three days later, my son called me, "Mommy, can I talk to you? I want to come home." He came home the next day. Thank you, Jesus!

Sometimes, abstaining from food is not easy. Our bellies scream, "Feed me!" We have headaches, dizziness and bad breath kicks in. To me, it is well worth it to say "No" to a piece of fried chicken to gain spiritual benefit. Fasting affects our bodies tremendously. Systematically, our bodies begin to clean themselves out on their own. The believer will decrease in size because pounds melt off quickly. Most people love and appreciate this benefit. The *most* important benefit of fasting is to get closer to God.

Fasting moves the believer from the outer court to the inner court. Fasting not only cleanses our natural bodies, it spiritually helps us get rid of distractions. Our minds are more alert, and our discernment is heightened to another level, if fasting is done correctly. Fasting kills the flesh, and the spirit man rules the body. This is the reason why most believers' spiritual hearing will be clearer whenever they fast.

In the Greek, fasting means "abstinence from food." The Hebrew root word means to "cover the mouth." Fasting is not only abstaining from food, but also other activities. When a fast is called, we must shut off all pleasurable activities in exchange for Bible reading and prayer. If reading the Word and prayer is not added to fasting, this is simply *dieting*. Sometimes, a believer misses a meal if they are too busy to eat and they call it a fast. Remember, biblical fasting is *intimacy*; the purpose of fasting is to go deeper with God. So, *real* biblical fasting is accompanied with prayer and Bible reading. The believer turns over their plate in exchange for intimacy with God.

In Daniel 10:3 we read, he *ate no pleasant bread, neither came flesh nor wine in his mouth, neither did he anoint himself at all, till the three whole weeks were fulfilled.* The Amplified Bible version of Daniel 10:3 says, ... *I did not anoint (refresh, groom) myself at all for the full three weeks.* What happened when Daniel fasted and prayed? According to the same chapter, a certain man came to Daniel to bring the answer to his prayer. *And he said unto me, O Daniel, a man greatly beloved ...* (Daniel 10:11). He was beloved of God. He was well pleased with his private sacrifices. God rewarded him.

When a fast is called, intimacy between a husband and his wife is sacrificed to hear and pursue the face of God. The Bible says that a husband and wife should agree to fast. *Do not deprive each other of sexual relations, unless you both agree to refrain from sexual intimacy for a limited time so you can give yourselves more completely to prayer. Afterward you should come together again so that Satan won't be able to tempt you because of your lack of self-control* (1 Corinthians 7:5, NLT). When a married couple commits themselves to God, totally sacrificing intimacy, they experience a greater level of intimacy with God. I have experienced this for myself. During one period of fasting, a couple days into my fast, I had not realized how sexual intimacy with my spouse could shift me out of a deeper place of intimacy with God.

Hearing God's voice was second nature. The weight of God's glory was tangible all over me and my spiritual discernment was magnified to another dimension. My husband and I never talked about setting aside intimacy before the fast began, and we were intimate. Where I was spiritually with God for those few days literally shifted in my body. I understood why 1 Corinthians 7:5 was written. When the believer is fasting—there is a place where the believer becomes one with God. Nothing separates them—no food, no distractions and no other interferences. They are one in mind and spirit with God! It is a special place designated *only* for God!

Through this time of intimacy, it broke my heart to end my fast. Walking in the glory of God is rewarding, which is why some believers choose living a fasted life before God. Much like Daniel in the Bible and in modern times, Kat Kerr. These great men and women of God have paid a price to live in the glory of God. Many people experience the glory pouring through these believers, but we do not know the cost! I heard Pastor Hinn say it takes him days to really break through his flesh before his spirit can become one with God. I can identify with Pastor Hinn, it may take six days of constant praying and fasting to break through distractions for my flesh to bask in the tangible presence of God.

During fasting, my spirit rules my soul and body. Hearing God's voice is easy and I can see clearly in the spirit. I have received many prophetic words, dreams, and visions during those times. One morning in my fasting time, God opened my eyes. I saw a huge angel dressed in pure white, standing in the corner of my bedroom holding two swords. I blinked my eyes and thought, "No way!" The Lord allowed my eyes to be opened in the spirit.

While fasting our sensitivity goes to a greater level, the answers become clearer. Also, the believer is full of unspeakable joy and laughter. This joy feels like a fountain of invisible water flowing from the inside out. When I am in this place in the spirit, nothing else matters. I just want more and more of Him. John describes being in the spirit, ... *[in special communication with the Holy Spirit and empowered to receive and record the revelation from Jesus Christ]* (Revelation 1:10, AMP). The Bible says, ...*walk in the Spirit, and ye shall not fulfill the lust of the flesh* (Galatians 5:16). We should live in the spirit, so we can be pleasing to God. When the believer is in the spirit, they become world changers.

Many generals in the faith like Dr. Myles Munroe and others experienced a high level of glory. Because they lived in the spirit. Dr. Munroe is in heaven now, and he left a rich inheritance for the church as it relates to kingdom living. He lived a life of prayer and fasting. God revealed to him a wealth of revelation for the body of Christ.

Kathryn Kuhlman also lived in this realm of the spirit. She did not weigh much and was light as a feather, yet lived her life fasted in the presence of God. There was no doubt— she was a carrier for the glory of God. In her meetings, she rarely laid hands on anyone, the glory rested on her wherever she went. I will speak more in-depth about the glory of God later in this book.

Fasting is the cure for disbelief. The Bible says the disciples asked the Lord why they could not heal the lunatic boy. Jesus told them that it was due to their unbelief. Jesus said to His disciples, *[But this kind of demon does not go out except by prayer and fasting]* (Matthew 17:21, AMP). Fasting and prayer work hand-in-hand to do wonderful things spiritually. I believe that demons attack believers who are fasting because the Holy Spirit within dominates as they fast. Consequently, when we are in contact with people their deliverance takes place.

One man of God said he fasted and prayed for forty days. When he went to the grocery store, demons began to manifest right in the aisle. Wow! Without touching or even praying for anyone, chains fell off the lives of individuals. His flesh was crucified, and the spirit man ruled. The anointing of God got stronger and yokes were destroyed.

Jesus is the perfect example to us all! In the fourth chapter of Matthew, Jesus was led into the wilderness by the Holy Spirit to be tempted by the devil. He depended on the Holy Spirit and the Word of God. What caught my attention was Satan appeared after He had fasted for forty days and forty nights. It was the most vulnerable time of His fast. Jesus overcame the temptation. After this fast, His earthly ministry began.

God uses fasting and prayer to release believers into their ministries. In Acts 13 the early church was worshipping the Lord through fasting. *The Holy Spirit said, Appoint Barnabas and Saul for the special work to which I have called them. So after more fasting and prayer, the men laid their hands on them and sent them on their way* (Acts 13:2–3, NLT). Even Paul and Barnabas … *appointed elders in every church. With prayer and fasting, they turned the elders over to the care of the Lord, in whom they put their trust* (Acts 14:23, NLT). The believer is released into destiny and their God-given purpose during a time of prayer and fasting.

While watching Christian television one day, Pastor Jentezen Franklin shared his testimony during a sermon. He confessed he never attended seminary, nor he did possess any degrees before pastoring. At an early age, he understood that he could not live off his parents' relationship with God. He had to develop his own relationship with God. He began to live a fasted life before God. He rented hotel rooms, locking himself away to pursue God. His secret faithfulness was honored by God. Now, he is the pastor of Kingdom Connection with campuses in many different locations. God rewards those who diligently seek him (Hebrew 11:6).

If you are suffering from spiritual bondage or bad habits and desire to break free, go on a fast. I had a season where I found myself on Facebook at least twenty times a day. I noticed how Facebook consumed my thoughts all day. It was easy to access on my phone—and I was on it a lot. I was led by the Holy Spirit into a fast. Not even thinking about my Facebook bad habits, I cut off all social activities to get closer to God and Facebook landed on top of my list.

The fast changed my appetite for Facebook. Yes, I still go on Facebook, but not like before. Some days, I may only log on two or three times, the desire is not there anymore. Take a leap of faith and break free from the bondage the enemy is trying to keep you in. His time has expired. It is time ... *to loose your bands of wickedness, to undo the heavy burdens, and to let you who are oppressed go free...*(Isaiah 58:6), and that every yoke in your life be broken.

In closing, fasting is not between you and anyone else. It is between you and the Lord. Fasting is intimacy taking you into a deeper place with God. This is a key to receiving manifestation! The Scripture says, *And rend your heart and not your garments...* in Joel 2:13. Fasting has nothing to do with the outside of man, like it did in the old covenant. It has everything to do with your heart. *Man looketh on the outward appearance, but the LORD looketh on the heart* (1 Samuel 16:7).

The Bible says, *And whenever you are fasting, do not look gloomy like the hypocrites, for they put on a sad and dismal face [like actors, discoloring their faces with ashes or dirt] so that their fasting may be seen by men. I assure you and most solemnly say to you, they [already] have their reward in full* (Matthew 6:16, AMP). We should not call any attention to ourselves during fasting. If we go around telling everyone it seems religious, and Jesus said we already have our reward. But real lasting rewards, do not come from man.

Fasting must be done in secret. God will reward your sacrifice and obedience to His voice. Think about this! No one in their right mind would have sexual intimacy with their spouse outside in a public place for the world to see. We must treat our intimacy with God in the same manner. Real and intimate fasting must be done in secret! God dwells in the secret place and our reward comes from Him only.

Chapter 7

Supernatural Encounter Through Intimacy

INTIMACY WITH GOD POSITIONS BELIEVERS to have supernatural encounters with Him. Jesus said, *Those who accept my commandments and obey them are the ones who love me. And because they love me, my Father will love them. And I will love them and reveal myself to each of them* (John 14:21, NLT). It is God's will to reveal Himself to those who love Him. If you love God, He wants to reveal Himself to you.

Jesus has appeared to many non-believers and believers alike. I heard a testimony on a Christian television network of an ex-Muslim who was about to kill himself. He was going through hardship and saw no way out. One day, he got into his car with plans to drive off a cliff, then Jesus showed up in his vehicle, and today he is saved.

On the contrary in Genesis 28, Jacob had been running from his brother Esau who stole his birthright. While on the run, he had an encounter with God. *As he slept, he dreamed of a stairway that reached from the earth up to heaven. And he saw the angels of God going up and down the stairway. At the top of the stairway stood the LORD, and he said, I am the Lord, the God of your grandfather Abraham, and the God of your father, Isaac. The ground you are lying on belongs to you. I am giving it to you and your descendants* (Genesis 28:12–13, NLT). The Lord recommitted to Jacob the covenant He made with Abraham. In return, Jacob made a vow to commit himself to God. This encounter propelled Jacob into his destiny.

As believers, we have received a supernatural encounter with God upon accepting Christ as Savior and when we are intimate with Him daily, without even realizing it. *Blessed [joyful, nourished by God's goodness] are those who hunger and thirst for righteousness [those who actively seek right standing with God], for they will be [completely] satisfied* in (Matthew 5:6 AMP). God will satisfy our desire and thirst for an encounter with Him.

We should, *Make God the utmost and pleasure of our lives, and he will provide for us what we desire the most* (Psalm 37:4, TPT).

When delighting in God, He gives us our heart's desire (Psalm 37:4). Pastor Jesse Duplantis desired to have a supernatural encounter with God. He shared on the show, *Sid Roth's It's Supernatural,* that he was reading the Bible and saw how God showed Himself to people in His Word. He said, "Why doesn't He show Himself to me?" Then he read that … *God is no respecter of persons* (Acts 10:34). After reading this Scripture, he told God out loud, "I want to see you; I want to talk to you over and over again." He began to get into position by staying up in the night, expecting to see God come to him. One night, after receiving a prophetic word from the Lord, a strong wind blew in his bedroom with a bright light. Jesus walked in. He told him three times to turn around and look at Him. Pastor Duplantis never turned around and Jesus left his room. Every believer has access to supernatural encounters.

The word encounter means, according to the Merriam-Webster dictionary, "to come upon face-to-face. It means to come upon or experience especially unexpectedly."

I believe our intimacy with Him positions us to see His face. Moses and many others throughout Scripture had face-to-face encounters with the Lord. Sadly, many believers do not understand how it is possible for Jesus to appear to some people in the church. Some believers are persecuted for saying they had face-to-face encounters with God. These are the believers who think having such an encounter only happened during biblical times.

In the Book of Revelation, John had a face-to-face encounter with Jesus on an island called Patmos. John said, *And in the midst of the lampstands I saw someone like the Son of Man, dressed in a robe reaching to His feet, and with a golden sash wrapped around His chest. His head and His hair were white like white wool, [glistening white] like snow; and His [all-seeing] eyes were [flashing] like a flame of fire [piercing into my being]. His feet were like burnished [white-hot] bronze, refined in a furnace, and His voice was [powerful] like the sound of many waters. In His right hand He held seven stars, and from His mouth came a sharp two-edged sword [of judgment]; and His face [reflecting His majesty and the Shekinah glory] was like the sun shining in [all] its power [at midday]* (Revelation 1:13–16, AMP).

Furthermore, John saw an open door in heaven. The same voice he heard before, spoke to him like a trumpet blast. *The voice said, "Come up here, and I will show you what must happen after this"* (Revelation 4:1, NLT). Jesus told John to come up higher (into the third heaven) where God is. Jesus was getting ready to give John revelation of Himself and the end times. John could not receive it unless he went up into the third heaven. If the believer lives from heaven to earth, they will know what is on God's mind just like John did. God will begin to show them what is to come.

Similarly, Daniel lived his life in the secret place and had face-to-face encounters with the Lord. God also gave Daniel a glimpse of the Great Tribulation that is yet to come. This is how he was described in Daniel 10:5–6 (AMP), *I raised my eyes and looked, and behold, there was a certain man dressed in linen, whose loins were girded with [a belt of] pure gold of Uphaz. His body also was like beryl* [with a golden luster], *his face had the appearance of lightning, his eyes were like flaming torches, his arms and his feet like the gleam of burnished bronze, and the sound of his words was like the noise of a multitude [of people or the roaring of the sea]*. These two encounters are different in description, both Daniel and John experienced face-to-face encounters with Jesus.

I can somewhat relate to these face-to-face supernatural encounters. When I first received Jesus as personal Savior, the pastor led us into many corporate fasts throughout the year. During one fast, the Holy Spirit came to me in a night vision, forever changing my life. In my face-to-face encounter, the Holy Spirit robe was the way Apostle John described, as *glistening white* like snow. It was so bright that I could feel the glory of His presence throughout my entire body. He laid hands on my forehead and fire erupted all over my body. In the natural, I could not stay still in my bed when I experienced His power throughout my entire being. Besides salvation, it was the most powerful encounter in my entire life! Then, I looked at His face; it had a circular shape without eyes, nose, and mouth. My visitation with the Holy Spirit was electrifying!

Every single born-again believer has the encounter (testimony) of being translated whether we know it or not. Colossians 1:13 (NLT) says, *For he has rescued us from the kingdom of darkness and transferred (translated) us into the Kingdom of his dear Son ...*, it is the first translation that takes place in the life of a believer. The word "translated" in Greek is *methistemi*. It means "to transpose, transfer, and remove from one place to another. It means a change in situation or place." In the Merriam-Webster dictionary, it means "to bear, remove, or change from one place, state, form, or appearance to another."

The prophet Jeremiah was translated back in time. God showed him the destruction that took place after creation in Genesis 1:1. Jeremiah said, *I looked at the earth [in my vision], and behold, it was [as at the time of creation] formless and void; And to the heavens, and they had no light. I looked at the mountains, and behold, they were trembling, and all the hills moved back and forth. I looked, and behold, there was no man, and all the birds of the air had fled. I looked, and behold, the fertile land was a wilderness, and all its cities were pulled down Before the [presence of the] LORD, before the fierce anger* (Jeremiah 4:23–26, AMP).

In Acts 8:38 when Philip was finished baptizing the eunuch, the Bible says, *...And when they were come up out of the water, the Spirit of the Lord caught* (Greek, word for caught is *harpazo*, which means to seize, carry off by force or snatch out or way) *away Philip, that the eunuch saw him no more: and he went on his way rejoicing. But Philip was found at Azotus; and passing through he preached in all the cities, till he came to Caesarea* (Acts 39–40).

In these two verses, Philip was translated by the spirit of the Lord from his encounter with the eunuch to Azotus and eventually to Caesarea. The phrase, *caught up,* according to the Merriam-Webster dictionary means "to be conveyed from one place to another." Philip's encounter gave us a glimpse of the coming rapture of the church. *For the Lord himself shall descend from heaven with a shout, with the voice of the archangel, and with the trump of God: and the dead in Christ shall rise first: Then we which are alive and remain shall be caught up* (Greek, *harpazo,* which means to be seize, carry off by force or snatch out or away) *together with them in the clouds, to meet the Lord in the air: and so shall we ever be with the Lord* (1 Thessalonians 4:16–17). Believers will be caught up to meet Jesus in the air. Are you ready?

Any believer can be supernaturally translated back in time or to a future event by the spirit of God, much like Jeremiah and Philip. One woman of God in Nigeria was traveling in a minivan. And without warning the minivan filled with passengers was kidnapped and taken into a forest. The woman said people were screaming and crying in the forest. She stepped to the side, closed her eyes and began singing a worship song. Instantly, she was carried off by force. After opening her eyes, she was out of the forest at a military checkpoint! Wow! Supernatural indeed!

Some of these encounters come in visions or dreams by word of knowledge, which deals with the past or present. Also, through a word of wisdom, which tells of things to come in the future. This is my own testament of a night vision encounter by word of wisdom. One night, I had a vision about giving a sister in Christ a ride home. In the natural, I had no idea where she lived. In the vision, I saw the outside of her apartment in clear detail. Her apartment was located on the left inside the complex, and I parked my car on the right. Weeks later, this same sister in Christ asked for a ride home. By this time, I had forgotten all about that vision. When we pulled up by her apartment, I screamed like I was losing my mind. The outside looked *exactly* the way it did in my vision! The Lord allowed me to see her apartment in the spirit before seeing it in the natural.

During the Coronavirus disease (COVID-19) pandemic of 2020, when America was on lockdown, I stood in my kitchen one day asking the Holy Spirit out loud, "What can I do to assist people who are struggling with COVID-19?" I prayed daily on their behalf, but I wanted to do more to help! Then, one night I had a supernatural encounter in a dream.

In this vision, inside a large auditorium, there I was ministering to a number of people. When I was finished ministering the Word, I asked if anyone there needed healing from COVID-19? Several people stood up. As I walked around the room ministering to one person at a time, I laid my hands on their forehead and said, "Be healed in Jesus' name." To my left stood an

African American woman with one hand lifted, trying to get my attention. Before I could lay my hands on her, she said, "Command the demonic spirit of COVID-19 to come out of me, in the name of Jesus." After she finished talking, I laid my hands on her forehead and commanded the demonic spirit of COVID-19 to come out of her in Jesus' name. Then, she fell back in her chair.

I walked over to my left and a young girl who looked around sixteen years old stood up for prayer. As I was about to lay my hands on her forehead, she began coughing uncontrollably. It did not affect me; I could not feel any saliva droplets on me. I was not afraid and continued to lay hands on her forehead commanding the demonic spirit of COVID-19 to leave, in the name of Jesus. I made my way ministering to different people in the room, then I woke up.

A couple of days later, I had another vision. I was ministering to a young adult who needed deliverance. In this encounter, we were in an open area that looked like a street. I laid my hand on her head and commanded her to be loosed in the name of Jesus! When I finished speaking those words, she went down in the Holy Spirit. Then, I woke up.

I believe both encounters were not just ordinary visions. I believe people needed deliverance and the Lord used me to bring deliverance to them. I could literally feel the power of God being released to the people I was praying for.

Some may wonder, how is this possible? Remember, a man is a three-fold being: spirit, soul, and body (1 Thessalonian 5:23). The spirit of man is created in God's image and likeness (Genesis 1:26). We have God's spirit living on the inside, which allows us to be translated by our spirit. I wanted to share these encounters before I move on to another example of being transported back to the crucifixion age.

One night, after falling asleep I was transported thousands of years back to the city of Jerusalem. There I was inside a room with Jesus being nailed to the cross. I saw a white sheet stained with blood draped over Him. When they began to nail His hands to the cross, I ran out of the room. As the hammer hit the nail, the sound sent a shockwave through my entire body that I felt in the natural.

It was not my mind's imagination, I had a real encounter. I was there. I ran downstairs in the basement of the house curling up on the floor like a ball. The sound of the hammer hitting the nails on Jesus' hands and feet was unbearable. Jesus made absolutely no sound. I just could not bear to watch. A Roman soldier came downstairs where I was sitting; I knew he was a Roman solider by the brown leather sandals on his feet. He picked me up and carried me back to the scene. Suddenly, I was transported on the street where Jesus had walked after taking thirty-nine stripes on His body. The street was bathed with blood, as if someone had just slaughtered an animal. People were lined up in the streets. There was darkness and stillness in the air that could be felt and seen. Then, I was taken back to the scene of Jesus being nailed to the cross.

I woke up with the sound of the hammer hitting the nail and my heart beating fast. A new sense of God's love for me as a born-again believer was birthed that morning. I realized I did not love Him first. He loved me even through my sins. His love was proved when Jesus gave His life for me (Romans 5:8). After this encounter with true love, my life was changed.

Chapter 8

Releasing the Anointing and Presence of God

Daily intimacy with the Holy Spirit is the secret to walking in great power. The more time a believer spends with God, the more powerful they will become. All power belongs to God, and we are not the source of it (1 Peter 5:11). Hence, the believer must lean and depend on God, the Source of life. Apart from Him, there is no true power. I say all "true power" is found with God. The enemy's power is counterfeit. Satan is already defeated and stripped of his power. The only power Satan has is the power we give to him.

In John 5:36 (ESV), Jesus said, *But the testimony that I have is greater than that of John. For the works that the Father has given me to accomplish, the very works that I am doing, bear witness about me that the Father has sent me.* The proof of Jesus' deity is demonstrated by His miraculous works. In John 6, we see a multitude following Jesus when they witnessed His miraculous signs as He healed the sick. Jesus had turned water into wine, healed the sick, raised the dead and cast out devils. Even greater works can be demonstrated through the lives of any spirit-filled believer.

I know several believers who have traveled all over the world to be in the presence of a great man or woman of God, who can demonstrate His miraculous power. In the Old Testament, the children of Israel had to go far to seek out the prophets for a word. God's spirit only rested on select people. Today, the kingdom of God is within the believer. Therefore, we can tap into God's presence anywhere we go. We have the Holy Spirit and whatever we thirst for cannot be satisfied from the outside. I have come across some believers who go from church to church, trying to find more of God. Their quest is usually short-lived. What they continue to look for can only be found through intimacy with God.

It is essential for the believer to know their union with Christ is complete. He is the head over every ruler and authority (Colossians 2:10, NLT). The spirit-filled believer already has the Holy Spirit's anointing dwelling inside. When they spend time in the secret place, God's presence flows outwardly, and people coming in contact with them will experience His presence and power.

The Bible says, *His brightness is like the sunlight; He has [bright] rays flashing from His hand, and there [in the sunlike splendor] is the hiding place of His power* (Habakkuk 3:4, AMP). The virtue of God is found in His presence. The more a believer is hidden in the secret place with the Father, the more God's power is manifested through them. All believers can partake, only a few will walk in great magnitude like Moses.

The Bible says Moses went on Mount Sinai in the Lord's presence for forty days and forty nights more than once. He did not eat any food or drink any water, and the glory of the Lord filled up every fiber of his being. He received the Ten Commandments and wrote each one on stone tablets (Exodus 34:28). After Moses came down from Mount Sinai, the glory of God was shown on his face. The brightness was illuminated like the sun and Moses was affected by His glory.

The people of Israel would see the face of Moses, that the skin of Moses' face was shining. And Moses would put the veil over his face again, until he went in to speak with him (Exodus 34:35, ESV). Moses was a conduit used by God to perform great works. The people felt and experienced God's glory through Moses. The Lord's presence could be encountered, but could not be transferred to the people. Evil or darkness could not persevere in the presence of Moses. He was a carrier of the glory of God. Wherever God's presence is there is freedom.

I am reminded of the story in Luke 6:17–19, when multitudes came to hear Jesus and to be healed of their diseases. *And he came down with them, and stood in the plain, and the company of his disciples, and a great multitude of people out of all Judaea and Jerusalem, and from the sea coast of Tyre and Sidon, which came to hear him, and to be healed of their diseases; And they that were vexed with unclean spirits: and they were healed. And the whole multitude sought to touch him: for there went virtue* (Greek word for virtue is dunamis, which mean strength, power, and ability) *out of him, and healed them all.*

In this text, nothing was said about Jesus laying hands on them, nor did it say anything about Jesus calling out demons! Jesus merely showed up, and the sick were healed. No one was left sick. Power came out of Jesus. It is God's will that *all* be healed. Jesus paid the price for healing.

The woman who had an issue of blood for twelve years pushed her way through the crowd and touched the hem of Jesus' garment. And straightaway, the fountain of her blood dried up and she was healed from that plague. Jesus immediately felt virtue leave out of Him, and He asked, "Who touched my clothes?" (Mark 5:25–30). This woman stepped out on faith to receive the anointing of Jesus. This is the yoke-destroying anointing!

Every single believer received the anointing at the time of salvation. *The anointing that you received from him abides in you, and you have no need that anyone should teach you. But as his anointing teaches you about everything, and is true, and is no lie—just as it has taught you, abide in him* (1 John 2:27, ESV). The Greek word for anointing is *chrisma*, which means "anything smeared on." The ointment here refers to the Holy Spirit from which all the gifts flow. *But ye have an unction from the Holy One, and ye know all things* (1 John 2:20). The word "unction" in Greek is also *chrisma*, which is the anointing that comes with the Holy Spirit. This equips believers with all things necessary for salvation and living a Christian life. In the Old Testament oil symbolizes the Holy Spirit.

The testimony of my brother being healed came from the Holy Spirit's anointing released over him, and the migraines that plagued his life for years were destroyed. The anointing can be released from an individual's mouth, hands, handkerchief, and through the leading of the Holy Spirit. The Holy Spirit or anointing rests on believers for service. The Bible says, *But you will receive power and ability when the Holy Spirit comes upon (Greek word for upon is heos, which means on, at, before, over, to) you; and you will be My witnesses, [to tell people about Me] both in Jerusalem and in all Judea, and Samaria, and even to the ends of the earth* (Acts 1:8, AMP).

The anointing on an individual's life is for His witness in the earth. If we are not a demonstration of the power of God on earth, then we are poor witnesses for Christ. Also, Jesus said, *If I do not do* the works of My Father [that is, the miracles that only God could perform], then don't believe Me* (John 10:37, AMP). Do not believe anyone who says they are of God, but does not perform the works of the Father! A believer must be a demonstration of power to be a representation of Christ on earth.

The Word of God tells us, *As for you, the anointing [the special gift, the preparation] which you received from Him remains [permanently] in you, and you have no need for anyone to teach you. But just as His anointing teaches you [giving you insight through the presence of the Holy Spirit] about all things, and is true and is not a lie, and just as His anointing has taught you, you must remain in Him[being rooted in Him, knit to Him]* (1 John 2:27, AMP). Hence, the anointing has already prepared an individual to do what they have been called to do. The anointing of the Holy Spirit will teach and lead us to all that is true.

Moses had an intimate relationship with God. God trusted Moses to do whatever He instructed him to do. In fact, God showed us His love for Moses when He defended him after Miriam and Aaron spoke against Moses for marrying a Cushite woman. What really got my attention about this story is what the Lord said to them. He said, *"… If there is a prophet among you, I the LORD will make Myself known to him in a vision And I will speak to him in a dream. But it is not so with My servant Moses; He is entrusted and faithful in all My house. With him I speak mouth to mouth [directly], clearly and openly and not in riddles; And he beholds the form of the LORD. Why then were you not afraid to speak against My servant Moses?"* (Numbers 12:6–8, AMP). Thus, Moses knew the Lord better than any other prophet or person in his time. He had a distinctive relationship with God. When God wanted to destroy the children of Israel, Moses interceded—and God changed His mind.

In Numbers 11, Moses was overwhelmed with the complaining of the children of Israel. The children of Israel wanted meat, it made Moses so angry and aggravated that he went to God. God instructed him to gather seventy elders to be recognized as leaders of Israel. The Lord came down in the cloud and told Moses that He would transfer the spirit upon him to the seventy elders for them to bear a portion of the burden (Numbers 11:17–18, AMP). This is a great example of the yoke-destroying anointing being moved from one person to another. God transferred the anointing from Moses to the elders with special grace to serve the people.

Similarly, Elijah asked Elisha what he wanted from him before he was taken up by the chariot of fire. Elisha told Elijah to let a double portion of his spirit be upon him (2 Kings 2:9). When Elijah was taken up in a whirlwind, his mantle that represented the double-portion anointing fell from him. Elisha picked it up as a sign that he received a double portion from Elijah. This is another example of the anointing being transferred from person to person.

So what really is the anointing that God has placed on man? The Word of God says, *Now, it is God himself who has anointed us. And he is constantly strengthening both you and us in union with Christ. He knows we are his since he has also stamped his seal of love over our hearts and has given us the Holy Spirit like an engagement ring is given to a bride—a payment of the blessings to come!* (2 Corinthians 1:21–22, TPT). God has anointed and given us the Holy Spirit as a down payment.

When we look at 1 Corinthians 12:4–6 (NLT) which says, *There are different kinds of spiritual gifts, but the same Spirit is the source of them all. There are different kinds of service, but we serve the same Lord. God works in different ways, but it is the same God who does the work in all of us.* It is the same anointing that works in different ways. Besides this, when one believer anoints another believer for ministry, the believer who is laying hands is standing as Jesus. We are one with Christ as Jesus is, so are we in this world (1 John 4:17).

Jesus said, *The Spirit of the Lord is upon me, because he hath anointed me to preach the gospel to the poor; he hath sent me to heal the brokenhearted, to preach deliverance to the captive, and recovering of sight to the blind, to set at liberty them that are bruised, to preach the acceptable year of the Lord* (Luke 4:18–19). Wow! Jesus was anointed to serve people. He came to the earth fully loaded to do the will of His father.

In Acts 10:38, ... *God anointed* (Greek word for anointing is *chrio*, which means consecrating Jesus to the Messianic office, and furnishing him with the necessary powers for its administration) *Jesus of Nazareth with the Holy Ghost and with power, who went about doing good, and healing all that were oppressed* (harsh control over one, to use one's power against another to oppress one) *of the devil; for God was with him.* Jesus was filled with power and wherever He went on the earth, His anointing destroyed every yoke and brought glory to His Father.

Believers have been anointed for a specific assignment. The Holy Spirit distributes gifts as He sees fit. The Bible says, *For many are called, but few are chosen* (Matthew 22:14). There are different types of anointing. Some believers are anointed to preach, teach, sing, heal, worship or dance; some are anointed for deliverance or to have prosperity ministries. This is not an exhaustive list. Although the anointing is different, they all come from the same Spirit.

The proof of the pudding is in the eating! When a believer is anointed, demonstrations of who they are will follow. I am always in awe being in the presence of anointed believers. Tasha Cobbs Leonard is an anointed gospel singer. When she sings chains break and fall off the lives of people. She was anointed by God to sing.

The anointing on her life is evidence of what she has been called to do. The gifts that come with an anointing are the evidence of the believer's calling. *For the gifts and the calling of God are irrevocable* (Romans 11:29, ESV). Whether our gifts are used to glorify God or not, will not sway His decision to take them from us. Nevertheless, the anointing on a person's life can lift. We see this clearly in the life of King Saul. The anointing departed from Saul, he walked in disobedience, arrogance and pride (1 Samuel 16:14).

One of my favorite demonstrations of the anointing at work was when I attended a Pentecostal prayer conference in 2016. The prophet of God announced that it was time to cast out demons. The music changed and there was a male voice roaring like a lion. His voice made the hairs on my body stand at attention. My heart was beating fast. Next thing I knew, demons began to manifest within believers and non-believers alike, with screaming and movement of their bodies. I wondered where I was for a moment.

The pastor roaring like a lion was nicknamed, "demon buster." His voice filled the room with anointing, and unclean spirits stood no chance. The evil spirit in my friend's neighbor began to manifest; not even the woman's father could have stopped the anointing from working. She began to foam at the mouth and her eyes were rolling back in their sockets. Suddenly, the stages were filled with people being delivered from unclean spirits. The anointing did its job. It destroyed the yokes and brought freedom to God's people.

Another pastor with the same anointing for deliverance said she went downtown to a public park in the middle of a city. As she walked by one lady, the lady fell and began foaming at the mouth. Wow! Lord, let my presence be that powerful!

In Acts 5:15 (AMP), the Bible says, ... *They even carried their sick out into the streets and put them on cots and sleeping pads, so that when Peter came by at least his shadow might fall on one of them [with healing power].* The question is, what was in Peter's shadow? Just being in the presence of someone with a yoke-destroying anointing produces supernatural results. The anointing is power, strength and ability; it heals the sick and sets every captive free. Surely, the anointing on the life of any believer will destroy the yoke. However, an anointed individual will not feel the anointing every time. I believe it is essential to spend time in the secret place, so that His presence can be released wherever we go.

Not every believer chooses to be a supplier of His presence in the earth. God's presence richly dwells in believers and we should take part in releasing it. It can be released in our homes, schools, churches, marketplaces—wherever we set our feet. Choosing to become distributors of the Lord's presence transforms lives.

My husband and I have committed ourselves to lives of prayer. Our home is saturated with an altar of prayers. By faith, we believe the presence of the Lord lives in our home. At the time we got married we lived in Virginia Beach, Virginia. My husband was stationed at Norfolk, Virginia Naval Base. We belonged to a local church, and two sisters in the Lord came over to our house because a church brother got arrested for drug use.

Together we decided to pray and intercede for him. As we prayed, one sister passed out on the living room floor and began foaming at the mouth. Not realizing what was going on, we tried to get her up thinking she had been hurt. She was unconscious on the floor for about twenty minutes before the Holy Spirit brought back to my mind the testimony of another woman in our church that was delivered from a drug addiction. I recalled her telling me about the day that she was delivered. This woman remembered falling at the altar and after waking up, someone in the service told her that she was foaming at the mouth laid out at the altar. Immediately, I jumped up and screamed, "Robert, get the oil! She is being delivered on our living room floor!"

When you are young in the Lord, you know nothing about demons, and if you have a first encounter like this—the blood of Jesus is enough! I got the oil and I could not tell you how many times I laid my hands on her forehead pleading the blood. That demon came out right in the middle of my floor that evening. She finally came to her senses with no idea what had happened or why we were standing over her.

That young lady was delivered from that demon, but when the demon came out, we didn't know it needed someplace to go. It remained in our home. In our small two bedroom townhouse, the demon moved from the living room to the stairs that led to our upstairs bedrooms. As we walked up the stairs, we would sense that there was a spirit of heaviness located on the stairs, right next to our son's bedroom.

My husband and I couldn't go to sleep because we felt a spirit of fear lingering. Again, the Lord brought back to my remembrance another testimony of a woman of God who told me that when her sister got delivered from the spirit of suicide, when the demon came out of her, her mother had to spiritually clean the home by opening the windows and doors, anointing the house and commanding the demon to leave the house in Jesus' name.

Straightaway, we got up, opened all the windows and doors and we took anointed oil and anointed our entire house. Then, we commanded that devil to leave our home in the name of Jesus. We felt immediate results.

I did not understand for many years after, why God would allow this to happen to us when we were inexperienced. Sometimes, I felt we were not properly prepared to handle this, being young in our faith. The Holy Spirit reminded me that He had already prepared me long before this happened. He allowed my sisters in the faith to share their testimonies with me as one way to prepare me for what was to come.

Now the Lord is the Spirit, and *where the Spirit of the Lord is, there is liberty [emancipation from bondage, true freedom]* (2 Corinthians 3:17, AMP). My sister in Christ received her true deliverance from the devil's bondage. The spirit of the Lord dwelled in our home and the kingdom of God was in our midst.

Another thing I have learned over the years about the Lord's presence, it is extremely delicate and must be handled with care. Through watching Pastor Benny Hinn's meetings, I learned there must be a reverence and sensitivity when the presence of the Lord is in our midst. If anyone attempted to walk at the wrong time, Pastor Hinn would ask them to sit down. He understands how delicate the presence is. I believe today that the church lacks sensitivity to God's presence. When the presence of the Lord is in our midst, you will see believers walking, talking, and watching the clock. If the service goes beyond a certain time, some will get up and leave.

During worship service, if the praise and worship leader sings the wrong song, His presence will lift. To me, when the atmosphere is saturated with His presence, and a leader is not sensitive to the Holy Spirit, it is like throwing a wet blanket on His presence. The presence of the Lord functions like lighting a fire to a pile of dry leaves. The first match has been lit and placed on the pile of leaves. Fanning the flame is important to allow what has already been lit to expand into a bigger fire. Moreover, the leader must be sensitive to the Holy Spirit to mature the flame and take the church to another level of glory. Most worship experiences never leave the outer court because leaders are not sensitive to the spirit of the Lord.

Worship experiences should go from faith to faith, and from glory to glory. It is like climbing from one level to another. If we are in the spirit during the service, we will discern the atmosphere shifting to another level. If there is a hunger for His glory, then the body of believers will experience a greater level of His presence. Church bodies who are time- sensitive do not experience the fullness of God's presence because they try to fit Him into their own schedule.

In June 2015, I had experienced an extremely high level of His glory at a prayer conference in New York. I will remember this encounter for the rest of my life. The people of God came with a hunger and desperation for God's presence, and the atmosphere was ripe with His glory. We were all on one accord and went from faith to faith and glory to another glory. During the service, several people saw angelic hosts in the room. People walked in the conference from off the street uninvited and said, "I want to be saved."

Many desperate for God found themselves stretched out on the floor. I was one of the leaders in this meeting. I literally saw some people being filled with the Holy Spirit before my eyes without the laying on of hands. As I walked through the crowd, several people began foaming at the mouth and vomiting. People were being delivered without anyone laying hands on them. It was a Holy Spirit encounter I will *never* forget.

After the meeting was over, it took me at least three to four days to shift out of the glory. I felt extremely high with glory's weight all over my body. I never felt that way in my whole life. On the drive back to Maryland, it felt like I was floating in midair. My husband and I were not the only ones affected by this high level of glory. Many who attended this conference testified about the glory felt on their natural bodies. Heaven visited us that day. The heavens were opened, and we had a Holy Spirit hangover. It was incredible, unforgettable and life changing! Prior to having this meeting, our prayer group fasted and prayed for a visitation from God; and He rewarded our faithfulness. He showed up powerfully.

Every believer can desire a great level of anointing, but do you want it? If the answer is yes, what are you willing to give up in order to go up? As we know, no amount of money can buy the anointing, gifting or anything God can give us. Nor can any amount of works or self-effort be enough to earn His gifting and anointing. It comes through intimacy, fellowship, and relationship. He rewards us with His anointing at a greater level.

Most times in the body of Christ when we see someone anointed and gifted, we wish to be like them. We say, "Oh my, that preacher preached the message and the whole church was a wreck. Oh, how I wish to preach and teach like that!" We never saw their journey to get to that level. Some of us tell these powerful men and women of God, "Lay hands on me, and transfer what's on you, to me."

Still, we do not see the invested time in prayer, studying, fasting, living pure, using their faith, and devouring the Word to walk in that level of glory. We want the anointing, although we have no idea what they had to sacrifice. We see the glory, but we do not know their story! Every believer has the anointing and it can be released by any spirit-filled believer. If we desire to walk in His anointing on a greater level, we can simply pray and ask for it. Just like Mary said, "Do whatever he tells you" (John 2:5, ESV).

CHAPTER 9

OVERFLOW OF HIS PRESENCE

WHEN WE COMMIT OURSELVES TO spending time in the presence of the Lord—in the secret place—His presence inside of believers will overflow. I always wondered why some generals in the faith like Kenneth E. Hagin, Kathryn Kuhlman and Benny Hinn would swing their hands releasing power to a crowd of hungry believers who fell out on the floor. The first time I saw this, I thought, "Is this for real? Can believers cause other believers to fall out when the power is released? Is this possible?" Then, the Holy Spirit gave me a revelation through this illustration.

The anointing became greater in the lives of these born-again believers. They spent quality time with God. As said before, every believer received the Holy Spirit at the time of salvation. The evidence that He is in us can be seen by our fruit. Also, when believers are baptized in the Holy Spirit with the evidence of speaking in tongues, God releases His anointing on them for service. Two supplies of power create a higher level of glory. When we pay the price and spend time in fellowship with God, everywhere we go people experience the glory. Below is demonstration of the two supplies: the anointing that is on the inside comes together with the anointing that rests on the outside to create the overflow.

The Bible says, *Whoever believes in me, as Scripture has said, rivers of living water will flow from within them* (John 7:38, NIV). The rivers of living water this verse speaks about is the Holy Spirit and His overflow in the lives of the believers. The clear glass represents the believer after receiving salvation. The water bubbling over the top of the glass is the Holy Spirit. Next, the water being poured into the glass (as stated in the prior chapter) is spoken of in Acts 1:8. This is the Holy Spirit that comes on the believers for service.

When these generals come to the public, the weight of God's glory is tangible on their lives. They release it to all who come into their presence. Walking in this level of glory is not cheap. They paid the price by sitting in the secret place daily. The anointing and power of God is heightened at a greater level. So, when they are ministering on stage, it is out of the overflow of His glory like the clear glass. As mentioned before, this same overflow would cause people to be healed just from being in Peter's shadow (Acts 5:15). Obviously, Peter paid the price to walk in this level of glory.

As the world experiences this greater anointing on the lives of those who have committed themselves to being intimate at a higher level of glory, you cannot help but wonder if it is real. The answer is yes, it is real.

Many years ago, when my husband and I lived in Virginia Beach, we went to church with a man of God who thought Pastor Benny Hinn was a fake. Although he believed in miracles, he told us it was overrated how the people of God would fall under the power of God when the power was released. That is, until he had an encounter that made him a believer.

Pastor Hinn had a meeting in Virginia, so he volunteered to serve in security. He was close to seven feet in height and weighed between 280 to 300 pounds. He was standing by the stage, then suddenly, Pastor Hinn swung his hands and he fell to the ground. The power knocked him out for a while. The glory is nothing to play with!

Pastor Hinn testified about one of his meetings in Columbus, Ohio, at the World Harvest Church in 2011, saying that he had been in the Lord's presence all night. When he walked on stage, he said nothing. He did not sing or even lay his hands on anyone. The next thing he knew, forty-three people in wheelchairs came into his meeting for healing. They all got up from their wheelchairs— the minute he walked on stage. He said this happened before coming out to the meeting. Because he was in the secret place, the glory of God literally wrapped itself around him. Pastor Hinn said Jesus [Himself] came out on the platform with him, and his presence became God's presence. Powerful!

I often viewed some of the Holy Ghost filled meetings of the late Pastor Kenneth E. Hagin on YouTube. As Pastor Kenneth swung his hands, believers fell under the power of the Holy Spirit. Pastor Kenneth invested time in God's presence daily. His cup overflowed to the point that the Holy Spirit inside ran over and collided with the anointing God placed on him for service. He was anointed with oil; he was a conduit of God's glory.

The late Kathryn Kuhlman was also an example of this. When she walked into her meeting place, the presence of the Lord was released. Chains were broken off the lives of the people of God—just like that. People fell out under the presence of the Lord. Glory! Is this level of glory only for some believers? Absolutely not! Any born-again, spirit-filled believer willing to pay the price of spending time in the secret place can walk in a high level of glory.

Please understand that these generals did not get to this level overnight, and they did not get this level of anointing from simply being on stage. The presence and power they carried resulted from time invested in the secret place being faithful to God. They were witnesses to His power openly. What we experienced from them on stage was an overflow or surplus of what they did in secret, when no one was looking, but God.

This is how to tell if a believer is leading God's people from the overflow or their flesh. If any believer makes room in their schedules or daily routine for intimacy with God, just like these generals, what they do in secret will become tangible evidence on the pulpit or anywhere they go.

In one season of my life, I was so frustrated with the church services as I hungered for more. The church I attended was having church without the Holy Spirit. I enjoyed God's people while serving in ministry, and I loved the pastor, his wife and leadership—but I wanted *more*. For about three years, I asked the Holy Spirit how to pray for this church body and what to do. One day, He told me the church was mechanical.

Everything about this church service was mechanical. The Holy Spirit could not do anything extra, He was not invited in. Praise and worship consisted of three songs, and the praise and worship leaders could not lead the congregation into a free flow of songs or worship. I was not sure if they felt led or not. We sang about the Holy Spirit, but He was not welcomed to have His way. The Holy Spirit was not thought of or preached about. My expectation was high during this time, I hungered for more of God. Every time I left church there was an emptiness that did not go away.

In all my years in this congregation, there was one time in service the worship was high. One woman of God began to speak in tongues out loud, then we waited for the interpretation. Before she could finish, the pastor asked, "Can you be quiet so I can bring forth the word?" Then, I saw security guards moving toward the woman just in case she did not take heed to the pastor's words.

For a long time, I could not understand the flow of this congregation. Every time I went to church, I asked myself why I was there. Even if I had missed church on Sunday, I knew *exactly* what was happening at any given time. After a while, I did not want to go to this church, each time I left it was the same way that I came.

Then, the Lord began to deal with me! Little by little, He gave me this revelation. He revealed that I was expecting this church service that only lasted one to two hours, to fulfill my hunger for more of Him and it was *not* possible! He told me that my thirst could be only be quenched when I spent time with Him in the secret place.

I had the wrong idea in mind of what I was supposed to receive from church. I had an idea and desired more of God. However, this could only be found when I lived in the secret place. My eyes were on the wrong source for spiritual fulfillment. When the Holy Spirit opened my eyes, I was grateful. I probably would have gone from church to church, looking for a service to satisfy my hunger. Many believers do the same, and some leave the church where God has destined them to be in that season.

What I was looking for was *not* found in our church's worship team, pastors, or leaders. What I hungered for was found in the secret place of God. His promises are true. If we hunger and thirst after righteousness, we shall be filled (Matthew 5:6). I am filled because He lives in me and I can access His presence anytime.

I am not saying that having good church attendance is not important! Any believer willing to invest time daily in the presence of God can stay filled with Him. Having more of Him comes from having daily fellowship with the Holy Spirit on the inside!

Once we set foot in the church building, others will experience the overflow of His glory when they come into our presence! When we live in the presence of God daily, we are not only going to church to hear a life-changing word, testimonies, fellowship or be an encouragement. It is also to release His presence to others. What would the congregation be like, if ninety-five percent (95%) of the believers sat in the secret place with God daily? It would literally be heaven on earth. The overflow of His glory would fill our cities, nations, counties and services so much that non-believers down the street from the church would experience God's glory. It would be like the time of revival at Azusa Street. There would be no lack spiritually, mentally, physically, or financially.

Chapter 10

Discovering the Inner You

One day, I received a phone call from one woman of God. She said, "Sister Maxine, I make a lot of money on my job. My bills are all paid, I have money left over in the bank, but Sister Maxine I have a problem. Even though I am grateful to God for providing and blessing me with such a good job, I feel like something is missing in my life. There is a place within me that feels as though there is a yearning for something more, that I haven't discovered yet."

Maybe some of you can relate to how this woman of God felt! Money is no problem to you— and your bills are paid. However deep down inside, you know there is *more* that God has created you to do. It is crying out within you screaming, "Discover me!" I cannot tell you how many believers I have met like this woman with no idea what God is calling them to do on earth. They have no idea how to discover the deposit God has made inside of them. Nonetheless, they know something is missing.

Jesus said, *Yes, I am the vine; you are the branches. Those who remain in me, and I in them, will produce much fruit. For apart from me you can do nothing* (John 15:5, NLT). When intimate with God, not only do we bear fruit; we discover what He has placed in us before the foundation of the earth. We must be connected to the Source of life to function at our true potential. If we discover who we are on the inside, it will become a reality on the outside.

In one season of my life, I could relate to that woman of God. I had no idea what I was called to do on this earth. I had a nine-to-five job, and I felt empty. Waking up on Monday morning was difficult most times; I wished for more to do in life. I felt void of purpose and destiny. God had placed purpose and destiny inside of me, but I had no idea how to make the discovery. I needed to pay my bills, so I worked. I had no intimacy with God. Consequently, my life was mechanical—a pure drag. I heard about having purpose and destiny; I did not know it was possible for me. For many years, I thought about opening a childcare center. I figured since I worked for one, why not own one for myself? So, I settled for owning a childcare center and thought it was the one thing I could do.

I spent many years pursuing a bachelor's degree in early childhood education. During my final years of undergrad, I realized there was no way I was called to stand in front of a class and teach children. I could not even see myself doing it. It was not heartfelt. In the end, I went to graduation, walked down the aisle and never received my degree.

Some may think that I wasted many years and lots of money to pursue something that was unfulfilling. The money did not matter to me. What mattered to me was that I enjoyed what I did with all my heart. I wanted to find where I belonged. Sadly, it took a lot of time and money before I discovered what God had deposited on the inside. Sometimes, when we think it is wasted time, actually it is God's plan working together for our good.

I had many years of secret tears. I call them "secret tears" because even though I looked like I had it altogether, privately, there was a cry for intimacy with the Father. I just did not know it. In the early part of my marriage, my husband spent years trying to console and restore me. I felt isolated, lonely, rejected, and separated from everyone around me. I did not understand and wanted to be like everyone else. Even though I was married, I dealt with loneliness and rejection. My husband was there whenever he could be, yet there was a void in my life that I did not know how to fill. I thought since I was married, my husband would fill the void, but he could not.

I compared myself to everyone around me who spoke about the friendships they had growing up. I could not relate. My divine connection of friendships only lasted for a season. The few friendships God allowed me to have were either distant or just not enough. I even felt like an outsider around my earthly brothers and sisters, who seemed to be closer to each other.

I endured such a long season of craving friendships (people) that it consumed my whole life. I literally cried out to God daily, "Lord, send me some friends I can relate to. Lord, I need godly friends." I thought something was wrong with me. I was friendly to others, yet no response. In the churches we attended, I would pick out a few people I thought had the same spiritual hunger as me. I would imagine myself being in friendships with them and nothing came about. This went on for years. The isolation, loneliness and rejection were real. When someone came into my life for a season, I thought, "Oh yes, thank you, Jesus for hearing my prayers!" I opened myself quickly, allowing them into my inner circle. It did not take me long to find out I'd made a mistake and I ended up with a broken heart. The purpose of our divine connection is not for friendship, but ministry.

Little by little, the Lord revealed what was missing in my life. The Lord used my pastor, Pastor Cynthia while she taught my class at Victory Bible College. She said, "Sometimes, God separates us for a season because He has something great for us to do." That very day, the rejection and isolation I'd dealt with lifted bit by bit. Ultimately, I realized it was God setting me apart for a reason and a season.

I found these Scriptures that encouraged me and confirmed what my pastor said in class. *You have been set apart as holy to the LORD your God, and he has chosen you from all the nations of the earth to be his own special treasure* (Deuteronomy 14:2, NLT). If the prophet Jeremiah were alive today, he would probably confirm that he knows what I am talking about. God told him, *Before I formed you in the womb I knew you, before you were born I set you apart; I appointed you as a prophet to the nations* (Jeremiah 1:5, NIV).

Some of you reading this book probably can agree with me. All your life, you felt isolated and even dealt with rejection. Please know that God has set you apart for His own use and purpose. It is not God's will for us to feel isolated and rejected or bring harm. He wants to use you for His glory.

I had not yet discovered what would satisfy the void I felt on the inside. Having fellowship with people was important, and I was craving it. However, I discovered the *only* thing that could fill my void was intimacy with the Father. This deep longing of my soul crying out could only be satisfied in the secret place with God. It had to happen that way, so I could discover the real me. I could not make this discovery without being intimate with the Father!

Maybe you are single or married and can relate to being lonely. Maybe you are craving sex, drugs, people, or marriage. This craving can only be satisfied when you discover the "real" you inside. This discovery can only be made through intimacy with the Father.

Most people might say that it is normal to feel lonely if you are single; this is not true. Once purpose is discovered, go after it with all your heart to live a purposeful divine life. I thought that we had to find our own purpose, but this is untrue. Each individual discovers what God has already deposited inside before the foundation of the earth.

Here is how I discovered my divine purpose. One morning while leading a prayer on a prayer line, the Holy Spirit shifted my prayer to preaching. I was shocked! I did not know God had called me to be a preacher. The preacher in me was discovered, and after making this discovery, my life changed quickly. Today, I have a Bachelor of Arts in Religious Studies and so much more. Discovering what was on the inside made my life fruitful.

Whatever God has called us to do in this world, it will come to pass! Every investment God made will bear much fruit when we spend time with Him. This discovery changed the direction of my life, and I no longer crave friendships to meet a need. Life became significant due to my intimacy with God.

Whatever is in you will surface in the secret place of God. The Holy Spirit is the person revealing to the believer what the Father has deposited inside. In Revelation 1:1 (AMP), the Bible says, *This is the revelation of Jesus Christ [His unveiling of the divine mysteries], which God [the Father] gave to Him to show to His bond-servants (believers) the things which must soon take place [in their entirety];*

and He sent and communicated it by His angel (divine messenger) to His bond-servant John.

If we want to find out what is hidden in us, we must spend time with God in the secret place so that the Holy Spirit can reveal what the Father knows about us. Elohim is the creator of all things. Once we are connected to Him, there is nothing He will not reveal to us. The Holy Spirit will reveal things that we have never seen before, while dwelling in the secret place. We will begin to discover purpose and destiny from the Creator, who created us. I believe every human being was born with a specific calling on their life. Whether we use it to glorify God or not, we were born with it.

The Bible says, *For many are called (invited, summoned), but only few are chosen* (Matthew 22:14, AMP). God chose some believers to have a specific ministry and when we are intimate with Him conception happens. The word "conception" in Hebrew is *herown*, which means "pregnancy." God impregnates His children with ministry in the secret place.

When I discovered my call to preach, I did not walk around telling everyone about me being a preacher. No one at church knew about my call to preach for a while, I just did not feel led to announce it. Once we are anointed and called by God; He is the One responsible for exposing us in the right season. If leaders live in the spirit, they have an unction that gives them the ability to know all things (1 John 2:20). It was not my place to tell.

During that season of discovery, each morning I pushed my way into prayer with an international Pentecostal prayer ministry. The revelation came to me about conception and being pregnant by the Holy Spirit. It happened to me!

One day during a prayer conference in Orlando, Florida, a prophetess came up to me and said, "God said, you are six months pregnant." I looked at my stomach and said to myself, *This woman is a false prophetess because there is no way possible I could be six months pregnant and my stomach is this flat.* I said, "No way, I still have my period, haven't had any signs of pregnancy." If I were pregnant, I would have known for sure. I communicated with my husband about what was said and we both laughed just like Sarah in Genesis 18:12.

As time went on, we both forgot about what was spoken concerning the "pregnancy." Three months later, another prophetess who had never met me outside the prayer line prophesied to me. "God said, you are nine months pregnant," the prophetess said. After almost passing out, I thought nine months pregnant and about to give birth—I was not ready!

We had no baby clothes, crib, bottles, or Pampers! I had no idea that I could be pregnant *spiritually*. I almost said out loud, *Prophetess, you have got to be kidding me! There is no way. How is it that I am ready to give birth and in the natural there is nothing in my belly?* The Lord brought back what the first prophetess told me three months earlier in Florida. Then I realized, this was a spiritual pregnancy, not a natural one.

Still clueless, I had never heard of anyone being pregnant by the Holy Spirit except Mary, the mother of Jesus. Then, on the same prayer line, a pastor said God had impregnated me with ministry and get ready to give birth. Also, being pregnant with ministry was unknown to me. One thing I love about God is nothing He does is by accident.

Nine months pregnant with ministry, I knew the time to give birth drew near. My prayer life was extremely healthy from being part of a prayer ministry. Fasting and praying was second nature—not something done on occasion. Nevertheless, I submitted myself to God's will. Then, something amazing happened. My husband dreamed that we had a girl with really long, pretty hair.

Two to three years passed, and I still wondered how could it be possible? I asked the Holy Spirit to explain in Scripture and eventually, He revealed this to me. In Genesis 4:1 it says, *And Adam knew* (Hebrew word for knew is *yada* which means "to know by experience or to be acquainted with") *Eve his wife; and she conceived, and bare Cain, and said, I have gotten a man from the LORD*. Eve conceived when she had fellowship (intimacy) with her husband, Adam. Conception is made through intimacy.

Now, let us look at Jeremiah 1:5, God told Jeremiah, *Before I formed thee in the belly I knew* (The Hebrew word for knew is *yada* which means "to know by experience, to be acquainted with)" *thee; and before thou camest forth out of the womb I sanctified* (set apart) *thee, and I ordained thee a prophet unto the nations.* God *yada* Jeremiah before he was formed in his mother's womb. Jeremiah's calling was placed in his spirit before conception took place in the natural. Before Jeremiah was born, God had already set him apart to serve Him as a prophet.

God also revealed to me that when we are intimate with Him in the secret place, what is birthed from the spiritual world to the natural world comes through [spiritual] pregnancy. This is how "true" ministry from God is born on the earth. God is not human. He does not have sexual intercourse with humans. God is a spirit, and He only gives birth to spirit. *That which is born of flesh is flesh, and that which is born of the Spirit is spirit* (John 3:6).

When we are intimate with God, He deposits a spiritual seed (Greek word for seed is *sperma,* which means "something that is sown") in us. This is how we become pregnant with ministry. Intimacy with the Father is the vehicle God uses to bring forth what is in the spiritual world, to the natural world. When the believer has a daily prayer life, the *sperma* grows from one stage to another. It is a spiritual pregnancy—not natural.

The Holy Spirit revealed to me, if the believer stops intimacy with God before giving birth, the *sperma* becomes stillborn. Sometimes, when the individual goes ahead of God launching their ministries before the baby grows to full term, they give birth to premature babies. I believe Jesus coming to the earth is a scriptural example of God impregnating His children with ministry. No, God does *not* impregnate us with baby Jesus!

That was the Virgin Mary's earthly calling. Mary was the human God used to bring forth Jesus, who is God in the flesh, to the earth. Spiritually speaking, the process of sowing a seed inside of the believer for ministry is the same concept as Mary being impregnated by the Holy Spirit. God impregnates us during intimacy with one *sperma* and that one seed multiplies into thousands—sometimes millions of souls won through that ministry.

Just like Mary, I was pregnant by the Holy Spirit with ministry. Unlike Mary who had spiritual midwives on earth, the Lord used my own praying and fasting (intimacy) to bring to pass what He had sown on the inside of me. Wow!

This is the process of sowing and reaping. The Word of God says, *While the earth remains, seedtime and harvest ... shall not cease* (Genesis 8:22, NKJV). Jesus was the first seed sown and every born-again believer is part of the harvest. *When you put a seed into the ground, it doesn't grow into a plant unless it dies first* (1 Corinthians 15:36, NLT). Everything God does has sowing and reaping wrapped up in it.

My pastors always talked about when they first started ministry. They would pray every Friday night in their basement. During that time, the Holy Spirit impregnated them with the ministry they have today. They are pastors of one church in eight different locations and counting! The Holy Spirit revealed to me that intimacy is the means of transportation necessary to birth [forth] the will of God in the earth. A strong, fruitful ministry is birthed and sustained through prayer.

I also believe that when taking any ministry or business to another dimension, intimacy is essential, the will of God for that ministry or business is already written. One must pray to bring what is already in the spirit to the natural world.

The Lord had called me into twenty-one days of fasting, and I did not realize that three of my sisters in Christ started fasting at that same time. We came together to pray daily for twenty-one days nonstop. When the fast was over, the Meeting Place was born.

The Meeting Place is a prayer ministry, where the saints of God come together Monday through Friday to pray and encourage each other. If the Holy Spirit had told me before that this was going to be the case, I would have probably said, "No, thanks." I was not interested in starting my own ministry. It happened quickly, it caught me off guard. Just like that, I was leading the people of God into prayer daily.

Intimacy with God in Me

My first year in the Meeting Place, I cried like a baby. Giving birth to this new baby I felt alone. With no idea what to do, I would wake up and prepare myself to lead the people. I would cry out, "Lord, I need help. Please send me help!" There was no one who could relate to my feelings at the time. The Holy Spirit had me completely dependent upon Him. When I felt like giving up, the Holy Spirit kept me going.

During the first three years, the Holy Spirit taught me to sit in the secret place with His presence daily. He taught me that if I plugged into Him—I would lead people out of His overflow. And before going on the line, I needed to wake up earlier to connect with Him to become an effective leader.

Still, I began asking Him for a mentor. Someone who could answer questions about ministry, pray for me and understand my challenges while leading. For days, I waited for a response. One morning after waking up, I heard the voice of God saying, "Wasn't I here to give you answers to all the questions you have asked me so far?" Then, He asked, "Who am I to you?" Then, I was reminded of the story in 1 Samuel 8:5-7, when Israel requested a king. The Lord told Samuel that they were not rejecting him; they were rejecting God as their King. Hearing this response shocked me. I did not like it, but understood it. I had to trust His leading. God led me the entire time; He wanted to be my mentor. God wanted me to totally depend on Him and just like the children of Israel, I wanted more. In that season of my life, I learned how to solely depend upon the Holy Spirit. It was critical for my survival. It is God who gives us His power to accomplish His calling.

If you have no idea what your calling is in the kingdom or maybe you know but have no idea how to start, I want to encourage you to sit in the secret place with God. Intimacy is the missing link in your life. Ministries are birthed in the secret place. Spend time with God to discover what dwells inside of you, there is so much that has yet to be discovered.

Pray and ask God to give you the desire to seek His face. One year from today, you will not recognize yourself. Some days, I still have to pinch myself. It is hard to believe that my life has taken this shift. When I wake up in the morning, I no longer feel lonely, rejected, empty or crave people. God has filled the void in my life with His presence!

As you begin to discover the real you, ignore the opinions of other people. Many may criticize you when they do not understand the things of God. People may look at you in disapproval, but soon they will see your fruit and know that there is a God living inside you.

Chapter 11

Intimacy Gives Us the Ability to Be Bold

ONE DAY, I HAD AN encounter with a lady in Walmart. She had one foot propped up on a knee-scooter pushing herself slowly. She had just finished working, and I felt led to stop and speak to her. I am so glad that I did; it was her last day on her job for a while. The next day, she was going to have maybe six or seven surgeries to repair her severely injured foot. I felt the spirit of boldness all over me when I asked to pray for her. As I prayed, my faith was released for divine healing. "You will have *no more* surgeries, and this is going to be a success. It will be your last time having this, in the name of Jesus," I boldly declared. When I was finished speaking, she said, "I don't know how that is going to happen, the doctors said I need more surgeries to repair my foot." I declared again. "No more surgeries in the name of Jesus!" A couple of months passed, and I ran into her again at Walmart. She was pushing a regular shopping cart walking normally. Thank you, Jesus for your goodness! That day, I realized once boldness is released supernatural results manifest as the outcome.

The word "boldness" in Greek is *parrhesia*. It means, freedom in speaking, unreservedness in speech, openly frank, free, fearless, and confident. Look at the life of Jesus, He was an example of boldness as He walked the earth. Although He was bold, He demonstrated a great deal of self-control. He only spoke when the Father spoke to Him. He was not afraid of anything or anyone and spoke the Word everywhere.

In the Book of Acts, there are many great examples of boldness in the lives of the first apostles. Many paid the price with their lives for the gospel's sake. They did not back down and persisted in the face of difficulties. They were fearless when mobs came against them because they were filled with the power of the Holy Spirit.

The Apostle Paul is a great example of someone with audacious faith allowing him to take bold risks. Paul exhibited supernatural boldness while he spread the gospel throughout the world. He was a man of God who prayed and kept himself encouraged in every situation. He was a true example of an intercessor praying for believers everywhere. While imprisoned, Paul was constantly in prayer and penned most of the New

Testament, including the Book of Philippians— which is a book of joy.

Apostle Paul knew what it meant to be in physical bondage and still have joy. He communed with God. When he was writing letters to believers, Paul would end each letter with prayers. He asked believers to pray that his faith would remain strong while he pressed forward to do the work of God. Paul's intimacy with God kept him going despite what he had to endure; it gave him the ability to be bold as a lion while sharing the good news of Christ.

Paul received his calling to preach the gospel to the Gentiles. God revealed a divine mystery to him. The Gentiles were co-heirs, members of the same body and partakers of the promise in Christ Jesus through the gospel (Ephesians 3:6). Apostle Paul considered himself to be a prisoner of Jesus Christ. He was tremendously persecuted for this message; but he did not back down. He preached with boldness wherever he was sent.

When Paul and Barnabas were on their first missionary journey, they went to the seaport of Seleucia and made contact with a false prophet named Bar-Jesus. Paul was filled with the Holy Spirit, who gave him great boldness. He looked at Bar-Jesus and said, *You son of the devil, full of every sort of deceit and fraud, and enemy of all that is good! Will you never stop perverting the true ways of the Lord? Watch now, for the Lord has laid his hand of punishment upon you, and you will be struck blind. You will not see the sunlight for some time. Instantly mist and darkness came over the man's eyes, and he began groping around begging for someone to take his hand and lead him* (Acts 13:10–11, NLT). Wow! Many might say this was too harsh, however, Paul was filled with the Holy Spirit, which enabled him to release words with boldness.

I was watching Prophet Alph Lukau of AMI in South Africa, and a witch came into the church service. The man of God picked it up in the spirit realm and located her without anyone saying a word. When he approached her, the witch said that she was sent by her master to disrupt the service. The man of God asked her to repent and accept Jesus as her personal Savior. She refused. Then he said, "I am giving you to the count of seven to repent," and she refused again. Just like Apostle Paul, Prophet Lukau said, "Then your eyes will now be blind until you have repented." I have never seen this before in the natural! What came next had me shaken to my core. Immediately, she began crying and rubbing her eyes. She said, "I can't see, I can't see!"

The Book of Acts came alive again, right before my eyes. Thank God for grace and mercy. The witch cried out in repentance and received Jesus as her personal Savior. The man of God laid hands on her eyes and her sight returned. These men of God do not have any power in their own strength. The Holy Spirit is the Source of their power. Any believer filled with the Holy Spirit can release what Jesus has already made available to them.

The message God gave Paul to preach came with precaution. Can you imagine Paul and his companions walking into synagogues with Jews who only believed in what was taught for generations, telling them that they received another revelation? The Jews considered these doctrines to be blasphemous. Paul did not let that stop him from preaching revelation with boldness while being severely persecuted.

When Paul and Barnabas were in Lystra and Derbe preaching to the people, they stoned Paul and dragged him out of town. The people thought he was dead. As the believers gathered around him, he got up and went back into the town—then left for Derbe the next day (Acts 14:19–20). What? They stoned and dragged him out of the town half dead? Then he got up and went back into the *same* town? Jesus! Paul was very courageous. He knew his assignment to the body of Christ— and he was willing to die to fulfill it.

In Acts 21, when Paul landed at the harbor of Tyre, some believers who prophesied through the Holy Spirit said Paul should not go to Jerusalem. Eventually, confirmation came to Paul that he should not go to Jerusalem from a man named Agabus. Agabus had the gift of prophecy. He went over to Paul took his belt, bound his feet and hands with it and said, *The Holy Spirit declares, so shall the owner of this belt be bound by the Jewish leaders in Jerusalem and turned over to the Gentiles* (Acts 21:11). After this, the local believers begged Paul not to go to Jerusalem due to impending danger. Despite, the warning from the Holy Spirit, he said his farewells to the people and proceeded to Jerusalem.

The danger ahead did not slow him down from what he believed. He placed sharing the gospel before his own life. Paul was free of fear, filled with confidence and courage. He asked the believers, "*Why all this weeping? You are breaking my heart! I am ready not only to be jailed at Jerusalem but even to die for the sake of the Lord Jesus*" (Acts 21:13, NLT). Wow!

In Paul's letter to Timothy, he wrote, *As for me, my life has already been poured out as an offering to God. The time of my death is near. I have fought the good fight, I have finished the race, and I have remained faithful. And now the prize awaits me—the crown of righteousness, which the Lord, the righteous Judge, will give me on the day of his return. And the prize is not just for me but for all who eagerly look forward to his appearing* (2 Timothy 4:6–8, NLT). He laid down his life as a gift and offering to God. He looked forward to receiving his eternal reward for what he had done on this earth. I am sure that God rewarded Paul for his earthly assignment.

Stephen was also filled with faith, boldness, and the Holy Spirit. He stood before a council and boldly preached the Word of God before his death. He had audacious faith and did not back down from preaching the gospel, even if it meant paying with his life for what he believed. When he finished addressing the council, the Bible says, Stephen was dragged out of the city and stoned to death. Before he died, Stephen lifted his eyes to heaven and prayed, *Lord Jesus, receive my spirit … Lord, don't charge them with this sin!* (Acts 7:58–59, NLT).

Maybe you are still wondering, how did these disciples become so bold? The answer again is the Holy Spirit, prayer, and faith. Even in today's world, we hear stories of those being martyred for the faith. This does not happen much in America, currently. But, it is the fate of believers living overseas who boldly refuse to deny Jesus and oftentimes killed for their beliefs.

One of my sisters in the Lord shared with me that terrorists pulled over a bus in Kenya and asked the passengers for their passports. Then, the terrorists asked who was Christian? The people who were Christian said, "We are." Next, they commanded the believers to deny Jesus. One couple boldly declared, "No, we will not deny Jesus!" They were beheaded. Their audacious faith stood strong in the face of death.

Believers spending time in the secret place of God receive spiritual boldness. In the Book of Acts, believers often prayed to receive boldness. They were fearless while sharing the gospel in the face of danger knowing their lives were at risk. Refusing to back down, they were full of the Holy Spirit and spoke with confidence. *The members of the council were amazed when they saw the boldness of Peter and John, for they could see that they were ordinary men with no special training in the Scriptures. They also recognized them as men who had been with Jesus* (Acts 4:13, NLT).

Members of the council recognized Peter and John had something different. Both had been with Jesus. This is the key! There was a freedom that allowed them to speak the Word boldly. Although they had no prior education in the Scriptures.

Before coming to know Jesus as my personal Savior, I was always shy while growing up because of my stutter. I tried my best not to talk and thought opening my mouth would make people notice my stutter. When I came to know Jesus as Savior, witnessing was something I did not desire to do fearing no one would understand me. When God healed me from stuttering, I slowly came out of my shell. I had been commissioned by God to share the good news.

Supernatural boldness manifested through me when I began speaking fluently in the Holy Spirit and spending time in His presence. Witnessing to the unsaved was not scary for me anymore. Whenever the Lord gave me a word for someone, no matter where I was, it was released in boldness. One day, I walked in Walmart and observed a woman at the jewelry counter. Under the Holy Spirit's prompting, I began sharing with her the good news of Jesus and she got saved.

In October 2017, I was traveling to a conference in Orlando, Florida. I had an encounter with a couple on the plane. Through this encounter, the Lord taught me that He is a God of divine connection. I was sitting in a window seat with two available seats next to me. A beautiful couple on their way to a weekend retreat sat right next to me. The noticeable tobacco smell circulated in the air as soon as the couple sat down. It was so strong that my nose started burning.

Conversation ensued, and the woman began talking about losing family members to cancer. I could tell she was still grieving over their deaths. After taking a deep breath I prayed within myself. In my effort to be an effective witness for Christ, I asked God to take my mind off the tobacco smell on her breath and in her clothes. Suddenly, the smell completely vanished and spiritual boldness took over. I was able to interact with this married couple without being distracted. She began to cry, and the love of God poured out of me. I threw my hands over a perfect stranger and held her tightly in my arms. The plane was full, although it felt like we were the only two sharing a moment of God's love. It did not matter to me who was around listening, this couple experienced God on a packed flight. Before the plane landed, this husband and wife received Jesus as their personal Savior in midair. Thank you, Jesus! God deserves all the praise over these souls. It is His Spirit working on the inside that allows me to be bold.

Eleven months after, out of the blue, I received a text that read, *Maxine it's me, the one who you prayed with on the plane. Can you please pray with me? Doctors said the cancer is back and I'm scared.* I felt honored that God would choose me to be a blessing to His daughter.

A heart of compassion and love was released as I prayed and believed God for the healing of this woman of God. If you need boldness, join me in this prayer from Acts 4 where Peter and John were just released from jail with threats that they were not to speak or teach in Jesus' name. They prayed, *And now, O Lord, hear their threats, and give us (me), your servant(s), great boldness in preaching your word. Stretch out your hand with healing power; may miraculous signs and wonders be done through the name of your holy servant Jesus* (Acts 4:29–30, NLT). Say, "I believe and receive it now!" After Peter and John finished praying, the meeting place shook and they were all filled with the Holy Spirit. Then they preached the Word of God with boldness, with miracles, signs and wonders following (Acts 4:31). The Holy Spirit empowered them with boldness when they asked for it in prayer.

Another morning after prayer, on my way to Walmart, I had purposed in my heart to be a witness for Christ. I prayed that God would divinely connect me with someone in need of Him. I opened my mouth and prayed in the Holy Spirit, then I began thanking God for it. I walked through the aisles in great expectation of connecting to someone who needed Jesus. As I approached the personal products aisle, I saw a woman who smelled like she drank an entire bottle of liquor and bathed herself in it. I began to speak to her about Jesus. "Oh no, not again," she said. I asked her what she meant by that statement. "Every time I come to Walmart, someone approaches me about Jesus."

Spiritual boldness came over me, and I began telling her that God loves her so much. And sent His only Son, Jesus to die for her. She broke down and began to cry. I moved in closer to hold her. The alcohol smell from her sweat rubbed all over me, then I held her even tighter.

After a few minutes, she admitted to being a backslider and said she had experienced "church" hurt. I told her again that God loved her. She asked, "How can He love me in this condition?"

"Regardless of where you are right now, God loves you so much. His love for you will *never* change," I responded. Next, I asked if she wanted to rededicate her life to Jesus. "How can He take me back if I am drunk?" she asked and looked at me, awaiting my response. "He will take you just as you are." Her response was, "No, I prefer to be sober when I give my life to Him again." I said, "Okay." Then, we exchanged numbers.

On my way home, the smell of liquor was all over my clothes and arms. I could not wait to get there and change clothes. I figured from the way my clothes smelled, my husband would probably smell it. But, it was all worth it.

Later on that day, she cried out to the Lord right in the comfort of her home. She gave her heart back to the Lord! Praise God! Thank you, Jesus!

Sometimes, believers are not willing to leave their comfort zone to reach others for Christ. Some of us get stuck inside the four walls of the church concerned with things that never mattered to God. Yet, souls are waiting to be brought into the kingdom. Jesus said, *The harvest truly is plentiful, but the laborers are few. Therefore pray the Lord of the harvest to send out laborers into His harvest* (Matthew 9:37–38, NKJV).

Boldness to be a witness comes from the Holy Spirit and every born-again believer has Him living on the inside. Boldness comes after we spend time in His presence. Only then are we able to preach (The Hebrew word for preach is *basar*, which means "proclaim, call and commission") the gospel with boldness and win the lost for Christ Jesus.

Before closing this chapter, I must point out a passage from the Book of Acts. The apostles preached the gospel boldly; the Bible says in part… *the church increased in number daily* (Acts 16:5). Can you imagine what would happen if a local assembly prayed together for God to give them boldness? The communities would never be the same again! Souls would be added to the church daily! Boldness brings increase into the kingdom of God. Believers must get involved in populating heaven, making sure souls miss hell.

Remember, the only thing we can take to heaven with us is another soul! We cannot take our big houses, expensive cars, the millions in the bank, fancy clothes, or anything material this world offers.

If you are timid, yet filled with the Holy Spirit, I want to tell you as a fellow believer that timidity is not an excuse. The Holy Spirit will make you as bold as a lion. Ask, believe, and receive. Take a step of faith and your life will never be the same again.

Chapter 12

Intimacy Positions Us to Hear God's Voice

THERE IS NO WAY TWO people can be in a successful relationship without good verbal communication. Healthy communication allows us to have healthy relationships. As a matter of fact, good communication builds intimacy between two individuals. I have come across many couples who experience the opposite. They are married without intimacy. They don't sleep in the same bed and lack communication—together, yet distant from each other.

Perhaps, it is due to hectic schedules, numerous disagreements, or life distractions. There is a cure for this. Someone in the relationship *must* make the first move to start the conversation. Intimacy is vital to any relationship. It brings couples together to get acquainted and deeply learn about each other. In the same way, when a believer feels like they cannot hear God speak, maybe they lack intimacy with the Holy Spirit. The reason I came to this conclusion is the Holy Spirit lives inside us, and we have unlimited access to Him. If we do not have daily conversations with Him, it is a strong indication that we are not intimate.

My sheep hear my voice, and I know them, and they follow me (John 10:27). Jesus also said, *I am the good shepherd: the good shepherd giveth his life for the sheep* (John 10:11). If you are a born-again believer, you are His sheep. The sheep hear the voice of the good shepherd.

The Three Voices Believers Hear

- *The voice of the Good Shepherd* – The voice of the Holy Spirit. It sounds like the characteristics of God. His voice promotes abundant (zoe) life.
- *The voice of flesh* – The voice of the flesh or emotion wants to control the person. The voice of the flesh only cares about me, myself and I. It desires the things of this world (1 John 2:16).
- *The voice of Satan* – Always opposes the voice of God and His character. The voice of Satan comes to steal, kill, and destroy (John 10:10).

One way to recognize the voice of the Holy Spirit is pay attention when He gives instruction. The voice of Satan almost always comes after, trying to contradict the voice of the Holy Spirit. The individual who hears the voice of God (deity) trains the five senses to know the difference between the voice of the flesh and the voice of Satan. If a believer hears God's voice clearly, they will be set apart from others. I am saying that because one word from the Lord can change a person's life forever.

Once we sit in the secret place of God daily, our spiritual ears are attuned to the frequency of the Holy Spirit. My cousin, Pastor Paula lives in the secret place of God. She shared this encounter with me. One morning after praying for the young people in her church, and in the community to be married, the Holy Spirit asked her a question. *"Have you ever seen a bride come out of this street?"* She'd lived on the same street for about thirty years, and could not recall any brides. Then, she found out about five young women who had children born out of wedlock, living with their children's fathers.

She searched out four neighbors on her street and asked if they had ever seen a bride from their street. All four answered no. Wow! No young woman had ever been married. She decided to wake up early and do something about it. She stood in the middle of her street and began to pray. She walked around the block taking authority over the prince of the air—who held that area hostage. Something supernatural occurred after she prayed. All five young women who were living with their children's fathers got married. And my cousin's daughter who is thirty years old, became the sixth bride. What a miracle!

This testimony taught me the Holy Spirit knows the answer to every single situation in our lives. He knows everything and wants to tell us—it is His promise to lead us to all truth. Our spiritual ears must be tuned into His voice to hear what we need to know. The Holy Spirit asked my cousin one question, and many lives were changed. Not only was my cousin's daughter set free—others were able to benefit from her sitting in the secret place with God.

It is important for believers to learn how to steward what the Holy Spirit is speaking to them. Sometimes when He gives a word, He will let the believer know what do. There are times He will lead the believer to only pray and intercede. The Holy Spirit does not want us to share everything. Years ago, the Holy Spirit revealed to me what I should pray for concerning an unsaved woman connected to my past.

He never told me to tell her; nevertheless, I repeated what the Holy Spirit had communicated to me. She did not understand spiritual things. Thus, I scared her away and our communication ended. Afterwards, I realized the Holy Spirit never meant for me to tell her. I was only supposed to pray for her deliverance. This experience taught me wisdom concerning what the Holy Spirit reveals to me. Since that day, whenever the Holy Spirit reveals something to me, I am not quick to share. Now, I am quick to pray and wait for His instruction.

While being on an international prayer line with other believers, I heard the Holy Spirit say, "There is someone on the line who is married. Every time she has sexual encounters with her husband, it is painful. Tell her the next time she has sex with him, there will be no pain." When I heard this word, I felt embarrassed for the woman of God, considering there was no privacy on a line with 150 people. God wanted to set the woman free. So, I stepped out on faith and released the word. Once it was released, the pastor on the line came forward and said, "Yes, Sister Maxine, I just spoke to the woman of God about this last night and she is on the line."

Once the prayer call ended, the woman of God called me to confirm. She told me that she had to go to the hospital because she began bleeding uncontrollably. After this word of knowledge from the Lord, she had no more pain. Her bleeding stopped and sexual intimacy with her husband was normal. I believe any spirit-filled believer can receive a word of knowledge and word of wisdom from the Holy Spirit resulting in lives being changed. God's voice is clear.

One morning, I was praying for the people on the line when I heard the Holy Spirit say, "Speak this on the line: 'If you only turn back, you are not coming back, you will not make it back'!" This word shook me to the core. It sounded like danger, but I knew someone needed it. By faith, I released the word. One woman of God came forward and said, "Sister Maxine, that word was specifically for me." She had decided to move back to her country; the Lord gave her this word to change the course of her life. She was about to make the biggest mistake that would have cost her everything. But God!

Be advised, if what we are hearing does not strengthen, encourage and comfort people (1 Corinthians 14:3), then we can conclude that we are tuned into the wrong frequency. I am *not* saying God does not give His people warnings concerning danger or upcoming judgment. If we never have prophecies to strengthen, encourage, and comfort God's people, then the believer may be hearing voices from the second heaven.

He spoke to free these women and give direction. When we spend time with God, our ability to hear goes to another level. Our spiritual ears are tuned into the mouth of God, and we always hear what He is saying. I also believe when we spend time with God in the secret place, we become extremely sensitive to His spirit and familiar with His voice.

God gave me this illustration. My husband and I have been married for nineteen years. Whenever he calls my name, I immediately recognize his voice from spending time with him daily and I am familiar with it. Acquainted in every way possible, we have been intimate for a long time. Hearing the voice of my husband is second nature to me. Even blindfolded, I would still be able to set his voice apart from others.

In the exact same way, when we are intimate with God daily, we grow accustomed to His voice. We live in the Holy of Holies and His voice becomes second nature to us. As soon as He calls our names, we know it is Him. The way He speaks is familiar, and we can never separate God's voice from His character and Word.

One woman of God asked me to pray for her. She was interested in dating a man who she said God told her they belonged together. After she spoke to him, this guy let her know that he was not interested and was in a relationship with someone else. She asked me to pray that he would change his mind. I thought for a moment; we serve a God of free will. I am not saying that this relationship might never happen. However, the voice of God will not speak to us and pressure others into doing something they do not want to do. He has given everyone the ability to choose. It is the character of God. I did not embarrass the woman and tell her that she did not hear from God. In time, she will learn how to recognize the voice of the Holy Spirit. After I hung up the phone, I said, "Lord, open her eyes to know the truth."

Believers must train themselves to correctly distinguish God's voice from the flesh and Satan. It is extremely important! Think about this. Sometimes, we spend years praying about a specific situation or circumstance. All we need from the Lord is one word, plus our obedience to His Word will change a person's life.

One Word + Obedience = Manifestation

Hearing from the Lord is not just for one believer. Every believer has the ability to hear from Him. Intimacy is key to cultivating our spiritual hearing.

The ability to hear the Holy Spirit's still, quiet voice is found when we are in the secret place. *After the earthquake, there was a fire. But that fire was not the LORD. After the fire, there was a quiet, gentle voice* (1 Kings 19:12, ERV).

I still recall my first encounter with the gentle voice of the Holy Spirit. When I first gave my heart to the Lord, I was living with my unsaved sister at the time.

I opened the refrigerator and as I picked up a container of food, I heard the still voice of the Holy Spirit say, "Put that down. If you eat it, it will cause distress between you and your sister." I knew for sure it was His voice because we were not seeing things eye to eye. If I had eaten her food, it would have caused distress between us. The fruit of love, kindness and goodness are found in this example. The fruit of His spirit is in His voice. See, the devil promotes discord. The devil would have said, *Go ahead, eat the food. It's her loss.* My sister and I would not have been at peace. So, I yielded to the voice of the Holy Spirit, put the container down, then walked away.

One Sunday, while still living with my sister, I was fully dressed for church. The enemy attempted to steal my joy before going. An argument began and my sister said, "Say one more word, and I will slap you!" She held her hand up to me. Then, the Holy Spirit spoke through me saying, "If you slap me, I will turn the next cheek" (Luke 6:29). I was surprised when those words came through my mouth. In that moment, I knew for sure the voice of God sounded like His Word.

I was a baby in Christ without much experience with His Word. He spoke through me with boldness. I knew my sister was surprised too. Later that day, as I sat down to analyze the situation, I held my cheeks and said, "Where did that come from?" Over the years, the voice of the Holy Spirit has become more fluent through me.

We can conclude that even though Samuel spent time in God's presence, he was not yet familiar with the voice of God in 1Samuel 3:4. The Bible says, God called him, and he did not recognize the His voice and thought Eli was calling him. Living in the temple, Samuel finally became accustomed to God's voice, serving God as prophet to nations and kings.

Hearing God on a higher level takes time, it does not happen overnight. While speaking to different people, God will speak to them through my mouth like He did for Jeremiah (Jeremiah 1:9).

During these encounters without even thinking about what to say, the Holy Spirit began filling my mouth with words.

Here are two encounters that occurred when I was having a meeting on the phone with my classmates. Suddenly, a word came out of my mouth for the entire class. I began to speak under the divine leading of the Holy Spirit. I did not plan it, nor did I hear it in my spirit; it just flowed out like water. When I was finished giving the word, I said to myself, *Oh no, where did that word come from? I did not mean to say that.* I could even discern that my classmates were taken aback by it. It was not a bad word, I just felt as though the Holy Spirit took charge. Later that night, I thought about the word and asked, "Father, what was that?"

The very next day at church, one of my classmates texted me and said, "Maxine, that word you spoke last night on the phone line was confirmed verbatim." I was shocked and overjoyed at the same time; I knew it did not come from me. It was even sweeter that God would confirm it.

Another supernatural encounter of the Lord putting His word in my mouth was when I was talking to a classmate on the phone. Without even thinking or hearing the voice of the Holy Spirit, I began giving him the answer to his prayers from that very morning. He said it was as if I was there listening to his prayer. I cannot tell you the countless times this has happened to me. I take *no* glory for myself; God gets all the glory and praise! The Holy Spirit revealed to me when this happens, our hearts become one with His. Out of the abundance of our hearts, the mouth will speak (Matthew 12:34).

While getting used to the Holy Spirit's voice, never be afraid to make a mistake concerning hearing Him. Sometimes, we may think that we heard from the Holy Spirit and did not. If it was a mistake, we should admit missing God and not give up. Every person who hears from God on a great level started out missing the mark. They did not give up and learned to hear His voice fluently.

When I first came to know Jesus, I made a vow to the Lord like Hannah. She vowed if God would give her a son, she would give him back to the Lord (1 Samuel 1:11). When I first read her amazing story of courage and faith, my faith went into action. My vow was a little different, I vowed to keep myself pure for my husband. I told God, I would not have sex or even date anyone. Before I was saved, I had a child out of wedlock. After going through many disappointments and heartbreaks in relationships, I came to Jesus wounded. I believed God for a husband and committed myself to purity.

Guess what happened? A counterfeit (Counterfeit according to the Merriam-Webster dictionary means made in imitation of something else with intent to deceive.) husband came into my life. He looked like the men that I dated in the past. Why? The devil heard my vow spoken in English. But, by the grace of God, I quickly rejected what the enemy had sent me. Within two years of being single, God honored my vow.

Many believers say the concept of making vows is from the Old Testament, it does not apply to our lives today. This is the wrong way of thinking. We make vows every day without realizing it; I am a living witness that God still answers vows. I kept myself pure and the Lord released my husband quickly.

He came to the church I attended with mutual friends. But, it wasn't love at first sight for either of us. One Sunday, the pastor gave an altar call; Robert was sitting in the row in front of me. I sensed by the Spirit he wanted to answer the altar call, but he didn't take a step. Then, I heard the Holy Spirit say, "Ask him if he wants you to walk with him to the altar." I stepped out on faith and asked. Immediately, he took a step and we walked towards the altar. That day in this little church in Virginia, Robert re-dedicated his heart back to the Lord. Please note, no way was I thinking, This is my husband. My spirit was rejoicing because another soul came back to Jesus! I never thought for a moment, this was my husband.

But, my friends began teasing or maybe they were prophesying, "Girl, that's a good man for you." But my response was, "Oh no, he is too dark." I began considering what I was used to. My preference was light-skinned men, but the Lord said in 1 Samuel 16:7 NIV, ... *The LORD does not look at the things people look at. People look at the outward appearance, but the LORD looks at the heart.* I wanted the Lord to choose for me, but I hadn't let go of my flesh and fully trusted Him to do what I asked Him to do because He sees the content of a man's heart.

Then every time I went to my friend's house he was there, and the Lord began to reveal his heart to me little by little. My friends didn't have a car at that time, so after work Robert would bring a change of clothes with him so he could take them anywhere they had to go. It didn't matter how long he had to wait.

My friend had an interview which lasted two hours; Robert sat in his truck and waited for my friend without saying a word or being upset. The Holy Spirit revealed to me the fruit of His spirit manifesting through his life, which got my attention.

When my friend shared this with me, I thought, Wow, this can't be right, and slowly my heart became tender toward him. I began to think, I've never met any man that does these kinds of things for anyone. Then, when my friends would say again, "Maxine, that's your husband," or "Girl, that's a good man for you," after a while I began to agree in my spirit without even saying a word. I began to fall in love with him, from the inside out. His dark skin wasn't a problem anymore, I felt drawn to being around him more.

One thing led to another, we began to communicate on the phone—it was not dating. This is the part I wanted to get to.

One night we were on the phone, and after speaking to him for a few days, I heard the still small voice clearly say to me, "This is he!" Yes, the Holy Spirit told me the man I was speaking to on the phone was my husband. Immediately, I began to laugh out loud—the same way Sarah laughed when the angel of the Lord said she would have a baby. I did not expect it to be so effortless. When I started laughing, my husband—who was not my husband at that time—asked, "What's so funny?" I responded, "I can't tell you, but you will find out for yourself."

We were married within six weeks after the Lord revealed this to me. Yes, you read that correctly. No dating. I just heard the voice of God and stepped out on faith. Naturally, people thought I was crazy because I did not know him well.

But, I am so glad I said yes! He is my soulmate for life. I love him to pieces. Beside, my relationship with Jesus, he is the best thing that has ever happened to me. Years earlier, I wrote down a list of qualities I was looking for in a man and God exceeded that list and gave me so much more. I am truly still in love with Robert.

I physically met Robert's family after we were already married. I can recall the first day I met his mother; as we pulled up in the vehicle, she was watering her flowers at the front of her home. The minute she saw our car and we stepped out and walked toward her, she held out both hands wide to my son and me, welcoming us with a huge hug. I felt the love of God extending towards us. I felt a sense of belonging, safety and peace. I felt like I had been part of the family for a while. That very day, I knew God was the author of it all. To Him be all the glory!

My reason for sharing our testimony is to tell you God's voice comes with His peace. I had great peace and knew the voice of truth would not lead me the wrong way. Recently we celebrated nineteen years of marriage and we are still going strong. Just like I said before, one word from the Lord will change our lives forever.

If you are single and reading this book, I want to tell you to pursue your relationship with God. Sit in His presence daily, so you can get familiar with His voice. The believer must have an ear to hear what the spirit of the Lord is saying. When you are presented with a prospective husband or wife, you will be tuned into the voice of God. If you are still not sure what God's voice sounds like, while dating go to someone strong in faith (like your pastor), who hears the voice of God. It is dangerous to marry someone the Bible describes as "unequally yoked."

What I have learned from this experience is the things of God are easy when the believer hears from the Lord. The life of the believer is much better when their spiritual ears are open to His voice. There are times I can truly hear His voice.

It is usually early morning between 3 a.m. and 6 a.m. when my mind is awake and my body is still in the bed. That's when God speaks to me. During this time, He gives me daily instructions and if I missed it the day before, He brings correction to me. Also, He gives me a life-changing word for the people of God. I use this time to go before the Lord asking the Holy Spirit questions about a situation I am dealing with.

One day, there was a misunderstanding during prayer. I did not know what made one woman of God want to leave her position. When I asked the Holy Spirit, He told me in great detail what the problem was about. By the time I spoke to this woman and told her what the Holy Spirit had revealed to me, it made her speechless. It was the exact issue. The voice of the Holy Spirit is important for all walks of life!

Another day, we were having trouble with our vacuum cleaner. I had been asking my husband to take it to the repair shop. It was pretty new, and I was almost certain they would fix it for a small price. After being in the secret place with the Holy Spirit, I heard the Holy Spirit say to me, "Tell Robert when he opens the vacuum, he will find the belt of the vacuum needs changing." Then, I said to Robert, "Baby, the Holy Spirit told me this morning when you open the vacuum, you will find the belt needs changing." When he opened the vacuum, the belt was busted in one spot and needed changing. When he changed the belt, the vacuum began to work again. I did not ask the Holy Spirit. He just told me! Thank you, Holy Spirit!

My mother had moved and misplaced her important documents, she looked everywhere and could not find them. I was on the phone with her and heard the Holy Spirit say, "Tell her to look in Alexis' closet." I told her. "Mama, look in Alexis' closet." My mom had not looked in the closet and told me that she did not feel led to invade my niece's privacy. About two or three months later, my niece found a bag inside her closet and handed it to my mom. When she opened it, all her missing documents were in there. Thank you, Holy Spirit!

This is only a tiny portion of real-life testimonies from the Holy Spirit speaking to me. Do you realize that anything you want to know He will tell you? Through intimacy you will be tune into the Holy Spirit's frequency.

Again, I believe many believers have difficulty hearing the still small voice of the Lord. It is not that they cannot hear—they are not willing to pay the price. They are too busy with life to spend time in God's presence. The believer must get rid of all distractions.

I would like to deal with the word *distraction*; this is how Satan tries to keep us away from the things of God. According to the Merriam-Webster dictionary, *distraction* is "an object that directs one's attention from something else." Have you ever experienced the following scenario? You decided to sit down to read your Bible or set time aside to pray. Either your phone will not stop ringing or a problem you are facing keeps replaying in your mind. You end up logging on to social media, or your children will not settle down. These are distractions, and tricks of the enemy. Please understand, I am not saying that your children are a distraction. The enemy will do whatever he can to take your mind off God.

If we are distracted in our minds, we will not be able to hear the still small voice of God or receive anything from the Lord. *A double minded man is unstable in all his ways. For let not that man think that he shall receive any thing of the Lord* (James 1:7–8). Martha was distracted by the big dinner she was preparing. She went to Jesus and said, *"Lord, doesn't it seem unfair to you that my sister just sits here while I do all the work? Tell her to come and help"* (Luke 10:40, NLT). Obviously, Martha thought cooking was more important than what her sister Mary was doing. Mary sat at Jesus' feet and listened to Him speaking. Mary preferred intimacy in the company of the Almighty God. Martha was caught up in distractions.

Most of our lives look like Martha's—full of unnecessary distractions. We get involved with busy schedules and have no time to sit at the feet of Jesus. Sometimes a good idea is not always a God idea. Saying *no* will make us more effective with what God has divinely given us to do and maybe fully commit to what He called us to do. There is no time for intimacy with Jesus—like Martha—

if we are distracted or busy. Satan does whatever he can to keep us from receiving from the Lord.

I heard this great testimony from a man of faith who had an encounter with Jesus. Jesus appeared and was giving him revelation. Abruptly, Satan showed up in the middle of his encounter with Jesus. Then, the man of God was unable to hear what Jesus said. He asked Jesus if He was going to do something about Satan. Jesus told him *no,* it was not His place. He gave that man the authority; he was responsible for dealing with Satan. Jesus was not. We must get rid of all distractions that Satan throws our way. We can do so by standing in authority, taking our place as kings and priests on the earth.

Most of us stay overwhelmed and hardly make time to spend with God. We want more things. Every time our jobs offer overtime, we jump on it—even if it means missing church or wearing ourselves down. This world has many distractions to take us away from God. The Bible says Satan is, … *the prince of the power of the air* (Ephesians 2:2). He uses the airways as a channel to distract the believers, such as social media and the news.

Some of God's people are political junkies. We feed ourselves twenty-four hours a day with Satan's agenda through the news and social media. Sadly, we spend more time listening to the enemy's lies, rather than listening to the Holy Spirit. Then, we wonder why our minds are full of confusion. Believers must not give into the enemy's distractions; it will be difficult to hear God.

Many great leaders invest in a place separate from where they live. They utilize that space to spend time tuning their spiritual ears to hear the Holy Spirit. They remove all distractions for a period to seek the Lord. Some sit in God's presence to revive their spirit and receive. The born-again believer has no excuse not to hear the voice of the Lord.

God speaks to His people in several ways. We focus on hearing the still small voice of the Lord by being in the secret place. Before closing out this chapter, I would like to discuss some other ways God speaks to His people.

Another way God speaks to His children is through their conscience. According to the Merriam-Webster dictionary, the word *conscience* is "an inner feeling or voice viewed as acting as a guide to the rightness or wrongness of one's behavior." In the Greek dictionary, the word *conscience* means "the soul as distinguishing between what is normally good and bad."

King Saul and his army were after David, the Bible says, ... *Saul went into a cave to relieve himself. But as it happened, David and his men were hiding farther back in that very cave! "Now's your opportunity!" David's men whispered to him. "Today the LORD is telling you, 'I will certainly put your enemy into your power, to do with as you wish.'" So, David crept forward and cut off a piece of the hem of*

Saul's robe. Something happened when David did this. *But then David's conscience began bothering him because he had cut Saul's robe* (1 Samuel 24:3–6, NLT). The Bible did not say that David heard the voice of the Lord. When David cut a piece of Saul's robe, God reminded him through his conscience (the inner feeling or voice) that Saul was His anointed one.

Here is another example. You went to Walmart, and the cashier forgot to scan the toilet paper on the bottom of your shopping cart. When you realized it, you were already in the parking lot celebrating. It felt like God blessed you. As you were about to drive away, your heart started to ache and beat fast. Then, your inner voice spoke, *what would Jesus do?* When our conscience speaks it plays over and over, until we fix the issue.

Next, God speaks to His people through situations or circumstances. The most important thing to remember is ask the Holy Spirit if what we are walking through is from Him or Satan? Please do not assume everything you walk through is from God.

Remember, when it is difficult to hear the Holy Spirit's small still voice, His Word will give us an encounter with the One, true living God. He will use people to speak into our lives. God used my pastors, countless times to give me direction *and* correction— right from the pulpit.

One day, my doorbell rang. It was UPS delivering a computer that my sister in New York bought for me from HSN. When opening the door, I was in tears. I did not ask her to buy it, I was just thankful that God loves me so much. I called my husband at work to share the good news with him and we gave God praise. When my excitement calmed down a little, I heard the Holy Spirit say, "It's not yours!"

"What? I believed you for it and you caused my sister to buy it for me and now you are saying it's not mine?" I asked. When my husband came home and looked at it I said, "Baby, the Lord said it's not ours." We both were wondering who it belonged to? Our excitement went from ten to zero. The Holy Spirit said, "I will show you who it belongs to." On Saturday, I went to Bible College and overheard a conversation between two of my classmates. One woman of God told another classmate that her computer crashed last night. I heard the Holy Spirit say, "That's who the computer belongs to."

The following Sunday morning, when I woke up, the Holy Spirit said, "Get the computer out of your house today. Today is the day." After the Holy Spirit spoke, I felt a sense of urgency. Before leaving for church I reminded my husband to put the new computer in our truck.

My pastor Tony was preparing to receive the offering at church. When he spoke, he confirmed exactly what God spoke to me. It was like he was watching and listening through my kitchen window. Therefore, I was honored to be the one giving. After church, the woman of God was in tears when we gave her the computer. She told me earlier that week, she was looking at the very *same* computer on HSN. God used my sister to be a blessing to her through me.

Next, God told me when He released me from working to stay home and write books. I came close to stepping out of God's will for my life by going to get a job. At times, I felt if I disregard the will of God for my life, God would reinforce His word to me again. So, we discussed it several times, and I would fill out applications—but still, I had no inner peace. My daughter brought home applications and I placed them on the living room table. The next day—which was Sunday—the Lord used my pastor Tony again to speak directly to us. Again, it was like he was listening to our conversation through our kitchen window.

"The enemy is trying to get you to move positions and let go of your faith. Don't move!" my pastor said during his teaching. I thought to myself, *How does he know I am thinking about working?* Then he said, "I didn't work for my three jets, God gave all of them to me. What you need, you can't work for. You must keep believing God!" Let me be clear. He was not saying that working was wrong. He said what I needed, *only* God could give it to me and to keep trusting God. Wow! You are talking about a right-now word!

Some of you reading this book have poor church attendance. How can you hear what God is saying without a preacher? (Romans 10:14). *I will give you shepherds after my own heart, who will guide you with knowledge and understanding* (Jeremiah 3:15, NLT). Choosing to stay in bed, rather than attend church service will cut off God's voice through our pastors. We forfeit the knowledge and understanding needed to guide us along life's journey.

Finally, God speaks to His people through inner pictures, visions, dreams, and many other ways. However He speaks to you, locate it in order to be tuned in with the Holy Spirit and get direction for your life.

Chapter 13

Intimacy Positions the Overcomer

I WANT TO FIRST GIVE double honor to Elder Gloria Corbett of Victory Bible College. She gave me the title for this chapter. I also want to thank her for the nuggets she dropped in my spirit while I was attending Victory Bible College. While speaking to our class, she said, "Intimacy with God gives us the ability to be overcomers." The spirit inside of me leaped for joy; I can bear witness and relate to what she said. If it were not for my life of intimacy with God, I do not know how I would have survived many difficult situations. It is God's grace and my position in the secret place that strengthened me to overcome every obstacle in my life.

Elder Gloria is a seasoned believer. She knows firsthand what she is talking about. She walked through many difficult trials in her life. She learned the secret of making it through victoriously. Today, in spite of it all, she still stands.

To the one who believes in Jesus, there are promises given to the believers in the church of Sardis (each believer). Revelation 3:4–5 (AMP) teaches us that every born-again believer, ... *overcomes [the world through believing that Jesus is the Son of God].* First, they will be dressed accordingly in white clothing (righteous). Secondly, He will never blot out their names from the Book of Life. Thirdly, He will confess and openly acknowledge their names before His Father and before angels, saying that he is one of Mine. Wow, these are some important promises to hold onto as overcomers.

The Bible declares, *For everyone born of God that is victorious and overcomes the world. This is the victory that has conquered and overcome the world—our [continuing, persistent] faith [in Jesus the Son of God]* (1 John 5:4, AMP). Who is the one who is victorious and overcomes the world? It is the one who believes and recognizes that Jesus is the Son of God. If you are a born-again believer in Jesus, then you have already overcome the world.

I believe an overcomer is birthed through revelation of their true identity in Christ Jesus. Once a believer receives this revelation, they begin to walk out what has been personally discovered, then the individual is an overcomer. We can say the transfer from the spiritual realm to the natural realm has been made. It is not enough to know, the believer must apply the truth to make the transfer to the world they live in.

Jesus has already overcome the world. The believer must receive (Greek word for receive is *lambano*, which means to "seize or remove") and apply it to their life. We must live on what has *already* been made available through the perfect sacrifice of Jesus' blood. The Word of God says, *For you died to this life, and your real life is hidden with Christ in God* (Colossians 3:3, NLT). When trouble comes our way, we are hidden in Christ Jesus and have already overcome. The believer must apply truth to their life and stand strong in victory.

For instance, the believer received a bad report from the doctors. The believer must stand in their true identity as an overcomer in Jesus. Since we are born-again, we have already conquered sickness and disease. The Bible says, *They conquered (overcame) him completely through the blood of the Lamb and the powerful word of his testimony. They triumphed because they did not love and cling to their own lives, even when faced with death* (Revelation 12:11, TPT). We can conclude that overcomers are blood-washed believers. Victorious through trials, walking without fear to come out with a testimony. Jesus has already overcome the world in our place (John 16:33). Hallelujah!

Sometimes, overcomers get knocked down by life's difficulties, but overcomers *never* stay down. They always get up and keep moving forward; it does not matter what happens!

To be an overcomer, the believer must trust and surrender all to God—and have daily encounters with His presence. The word *trust* is the Hebrew word *batah*, which means to "have confidence in or to be secure." *Surrender* means according to the Merriam-Webster dictionary, "to yield to the power, control, or possession of another upon." In other words, it means to let go, give up, or lay that thing burdening us at the feet of Jesus. We must let go of our situation and surrender everything to Him.

Overcomers know how to yield burdens to God; it is the only way we can come into a place of rest. In a resting place, we take our eyes off every situation faced, we know it does not belong to us—it belongs to God. And learning from experience the secret to making it through is a life of intimacy with God.

When walking through trials, overcomers hide in the secret place of Almighty God. In this place, we are sustained and kept safe. Thus, we can endure suffering or hardship as a good soldier of Christ Jesus and come out victorious (2 Timothy 2:3). When an overcomer comes into a place of intimacy with God—an exchange takes place. We exchange every problem with Him to become an agent of rest. Overcomers give God permission to work on our behalf. In exchange, we receive everything that God has available for us. Overcomers focus on what is above and not on what is happening around us. We can receive total peace, and unspeakable joy flows from the inside out. The fruit of joy is evident in the life of an overcomer. When nothing is funny, overcomers cannot help having outbursts of laughter coming from the depths of our bellies. Joy overflows from within. His joy is our strength (Nehemiah 8:10).

The children of Israel who came out of Egypt were not overcomers. They were not blood washed. While being tested in the desert, they began to murmur and complain against God. As a result, most of them died in the wilderness experience. They did not know how to let go, rest, surrender or trust God. Most did not receive God's promises because they did not trust Him to take care of them. But, there are many overcomers we can glean from in the Word.

Daniel fits the description of an overcomer. Even though Daniel was not blood washed, his life was a good example of an overcomer in his time. He did not just visit the secret place, he lived in God's secret place. When he faced a trial, he was victorious. Throughout his life, he prayed and got results. Whenever he went through something or faced trials, Daniel knew the safest place was in the presence of the Lord.

The administrator's high officers searched for fault in Daniel's government affairs, but they could not find any. He was an honorable man with great integrity, and his commitment to a life of prayer was evident. He was a highly respected man who was promoted and celebrated for it. They found fault through the rules of his religion; they knew Daniel's faithfulness to his God and that he prayed three times a day. These officials came up with a law that had great consequences if broken. It would restrict Daniel's prayer life.

Daniel was not afraid of any consequences. He did not change his prayer habits to please anyone. He continued to sit in the secret place daily. He had the ability to totally trust, surrender, and rest in God. The high officials found a reason to throw Daniel in the lion's den. Daniel needed a miracle and received it. God shut the mouths of the lions and Daniel was unharmed. He was able to overcome that trial.

Jonah is another person in the Bible who was not blood washed. He is another great example of an overcomer. In Jonah the first chapter, God told Jonah to go to Nineveh and announce judgment to the people for their wickedness. Instead of obeying the voice of the Lord, Jonah went the opposite direction and took a ship to Tarshish. The Lord caused a great storm and Jonah was chosen by lots to be thrown overboard. God arranged for a great fish to swallow Jonah and he remained in the fish's belly for three days and three nights.

In the second chapter, while Jonah was in the fish's belly, he prayed and said, *I cried out to the LORD in my great trouble, and he answered me. I called to you from the land of the dead and LORD, you heard me! You threw me into the ocean depths, and I sank down to the heart of the sea. The mighty waters engulfed me; I was buried beneath your wild and stormy waves. Then I said, 'O LORD, you have driven me from your presence. Yet I will look once more toward your holy Temple. I sank beneath the waves, and the water closed over me. Seaweed wrapped itself around my head* (Jonah 2:2–5, NLT). Just as David said, *… if I make my bed in hell, behold, thou art there* (Psalm 139:8). Jonah cried out to God for help, *then the LORD ordered the fish to spit Jonah out onto the beach* (Jonah 2:10, NLT).

In the third chapter of Jonah, after he was released from the fish's belly, Jonah obeyed God and spoke His word to the people of Nineveh. Jonah caused his own trouble; however, he knew what to do and where to go when he needed help. Jonah overcame his situation even though he had walked in disobedience! If God heard the cry of Jonah while he was in the fish's belly, He will hear your cry. Wherever you find yourself crying out to God, He will rescue you. The Bible says, *The righteous person faces many troubles, but the LORD comes to the rescue each time* (Psalm 34:19, NLT). Glory!

Finally, Apostle Paul is another great example of an overcomer. He was a blood washed, spirit filled believer who lived a life of intimacy with God. He was an exceptional leader who prayed his way through every situation he found himself in. He was a living example for all believers to follow. Before Paul's encounter with Jesus on the road to Damascus in Acts 9, he persecuted believers and put them in prison, but Paul the overcomer didn't reminisce on his past. He saw himself the way God sees him.

Paul said, *We have not done wrong to anyone or caused harm to anyone. And we have not cheated anyone* (2 Corinthians 7:2, ERV). He was free from the condemnation of his past.

Paul understood what it meant to be an overcomer; he demonstrated it in his personal life. He lay down his life to God in surrender. He committed his life to sharing the gospel at all costs. Paul overcame the world he lived in and he didn't dwell on his physical condition, only the spiritual. He wrote in Philippians 1:23–42 NLT, that he was *torn between two desires: I long to go and be with Christ, which would be far better for me. But for your sakes, it is better that I continue to live.*

Paul, the overcomer had joy in spite of what he was walking through. His fleshly circumstances did not slow or stop him from what he was called to do.

He endured hardship as a good soldier of Christ. He faced death, five times received thirty-nine lashes, three times beaten with rods, stoned, shipwrecked, spent a whole night and a day drifting at sea, traveled many long journeys, faced danger from rivers, robbers, faced danger in cities, deserts and on sea, been hungry and thirsty and many other difficult situations (2 Corinthians 2:23–27). Yet still, Paul rejoiced in the Lord his God; he said, *Even if I lose my life, pouring it out like a liquid offering to God…* (Philippians 2:17 NLT). Paul wrote most of the New Testament letters in prison, but he was a free man in the spirit. He lived his life as an overcomer because Jesus overcame over thousands of years ago in his place. Hallelujah!

Intimacy with God gives believers the ability to overcome offenses, hurt and pain. Believers are not exempt from offense. Jesus told His disciples, *It is impossible but that offences* (Greek meaning, "a trigger of a trap, snare, any impediment placed in the way and causing one to stumble or fall)" *will come: but woe unto him, through whom they come!* (Luke 17:1).

Overcomers will experience offense, hurt and pain; woe (warning) to the one who operates in the spirit of offense. The overcomer must know walking in offense is a trigger of a trap and its ultimate purpose is to remove us from the things of God.

I have learned the best way to overcome offense, hurt and pain is to run into the presence of the Lord. In His presence, the Father will give us the capacity to love difficult people and let -go of hurt, offense and pain. *He heals the brokenhearted And binds up their wounds [healing their pain and comforting their sorrow]* (Psalm 147:3, AMP). When we live in the presence of the Lord, the believer can throw their cares at the feet of Jesus. In return, He will heal our broken hearts, comfort us and give us the ability to let go of all hurt and pain. The minute offense comes our way, we must be honest with God—even though He already knows we are hurt.

Hence, we can offend the people that we hold dear without knowing it. Offense is not only about us being offended; it is about us being offensive to the people we love. It is not wise to get other people involved when we are offended. Offense will move from person to person. The reason this happens is because offense is a spirit—Satan himself. The best way to overcome offenses is to sit in the presence of God. When I am hurt, I come clean with God. I ask the Lord to mend my hurt, heal my heart and help me to forgive.

One morning before taking my feet off the bed, eyes still closed, I heard the Holy Spirit's voice whisper, "1 Peter 5:9." I reached for my phone and eagerly scrolled to find this verse in the New Living Translation version of the Bible. This is what I found, *Stand firm against him, and be strong in your faith. Remember that your family of believers all over the world are going through the same kind of suffering you are.* When I finished reading this verse, my heart began beating fast because I knew I was about to walk through something difficult. The Holy Spirit gave me this verse in order to prepare me for what was coming.

Later that very day, I received a call from a pastor on the international prayer line, where I was serving. She was accusing me of doing something I did not do. Even though the Holy Spirit had prepared me earlier that morning, my heart was broken into pieces and I was hurt. The enemy was telling me to run from the ministry, and not deal with the hurt. But, I knew God was not finished with me yet. What made matters worse was being asked to apologize before everyone in the prayer room for something I did not do. This was not something I was used to. It was way out of my comfort zone. It is easier for me to say "sorry" if it is my fault—this was new to me.

One morning, I cried out to God to help me, "God, I did not do it. My heart is broken, I am being accused of doing something I did not do. Lord, help me, I need you!" The Lord's voice replied, "What did I do when I was nailed to the cross?" After hearing this, it surprised me. I needed to walk through it. Even though heartbroken, I could not run from it and at the same time stand strong in faith. Every day, I felt God's strength as I walked though this short season.

The pastor told me to write my apology on paper and send it to her before going on the line to apologize. I didn't understand why, but I submitted myself to her authority and did what she asked. When I emailed my apology, what I believe came from my spirit, she edited it and sent it back to me and said, "No, say this instead." The morning of my apology, I woke early before going in the prayer room to sit in the secret place with Jehovah Shalom, the

Intimacy with God in Me

God of peace. I prayed in the spirit until I felt His supernatural peace come up all over me. When I was finished, I felt strengthen!

I boldly read the apology from the piece of paper that was given to me to the prayer room. Nevertheless, during my apology some of the attendees interrupted me and asked, "Sister Maxine, why are you apologizing, you didn't do anything wrong?" The pastor then asked the attendees to mute their lines and I continued my apology. When I was done, I felt His peace cover me like a blanket. I knew God was pleased and I felt growth. I was able to forgive, love and let go of my hurt. I continued serving in this ministry, until God released me. I was so thankful to walk through this trial; I learned where to go when my heart is broken and when offense tries to trap me. For any overcomer to walk in supernatural strength, we must stay in the presence of the Lord. In this place, we can be restored to "begin" again.

Chapter 14

The Believer Bears Fruit in the Secret Place

THE LIFE OF THE BELIEVER becomes fruitful when we live in His secret place with God. He tells us, *So you must remain in life-union with me, for I remain in life-union with you. For as a branch severed from the vine will not bear fruit, so your life will be fruitless unless you live your life intimately joined with mine. I am the sprouting vine and you're my branches. As you live in union with me as your source, fruitfulness will stream from within you—but when you live separated from me you are powerless. If a person is separated from me, he is discarded; such branches are gathered up and thrown into the fire to be burned. But if you live in life-union with me and if my words live powerfully within you—then you can ask whatever you desire, and it will be done. When your lives bear abundant fruit, you demonstrate that you are my mature disciples who glorify my Father!* (John 15:4–8, TPT). Oh wow!

These few verses from The Passion Translation tell us how the believer becomes fruitful. We bear fruit in our union with Christ Jesus. If we are not in union with Him, then we will not bear fruit. In other words, fruitfulness comes from fellowship. Apart from God, we can do nothing. Fruitfulness is the ability to bear fruit in every area of life including spirit, soul, body and financially. The only way this happens is we must keep ourselves plugged into the source to bear fruit. Jesus says that He is the vine that connects believers to the source of everything fruitful. When the believer spends time with Him, we cannot help but to become fruitful.

When we are connected to the Vine, the first fruit we begin to cultivate in the secret place is the fruit of His spirit. The character of God begins to develop from the inside out. In our contact with others, they experience the character of God. As an outcome, the branch of the believer begins to bear fruit.

Just the other day, one of my prayer partners said to me, "Sister Maxine, something happened to me without even thinking about it. My daughter is building a house and there was a problem with the person who is building the house. When I spoke to her, she was upset but what came out of my mouth was, 'All is well. Just trust God, everything will work out.' Peace came over me concerning what was going on, and I was able to encourage my daughter. This is a big change for me because I am usually worried right along with my family about every situation. But great peace came over me."

From this example, we see this woman of God bearing fruit—she is connected to the true Vine. If you are not exhibiting the fruit of His spirit, intimacy with God is missing. *If we claim that we share life with him, but keep walking in the realm of darkness, we're fooling ourselves and not living the truth. But if we keep living in the pure light that surrounds him, we share unbroken fellowship with one another, and the blood of Jesus, his Son, continually cleanses us from all sin* (1 John 1:6–7, TPT).

As we live in the light with God, His light shines through us. Intimacy with God changes the entire being of a believer's life. Once a believer makes the decision to dedicate their life to intimacy, everything changes. I have heard many testimonies from saints of God who say, "I was saved a long time ago; it's when I began to have daily intimacy with God that my life, business, ministry and finances began to prosper."

A woman of God came to the Meeting Place, and her life was a pure drag. She had no idea what her calling was in the body of Christ. Since then, God revealed a seer anointing on her life that manifests through dreams and visions. She is now a minister of the gospel impacting lives. Every time we talk, my soul is overjoyed with what God is doing in her life.

Without a shadow of a doubt, she made the right decision to pursue intimacy daily with God—and became fruitful.

More evidence of fruitfulness takes place when we are intimate with God in our minds, becoming one with Him. *But the one who is united and joined to the Lord is one spirit with Him* (1 Corinthians 6:17, AMP). This oneness is spirit, soul, and body—which encompasses the whole man. His thoughts become our thoughts. In Dr. Munroe's book on prayer, he called this "manifesting the thoughts of God." He said, "Our thoughts are intimate and what we say is an expression of His thoughts." I can see why this is true; as a man thinks, that is who he is (Proverbs 23:7). Dr. Munroe said, "God's desire is not to speak to us, but to think through us." It is like this whenever we have a thought. Our thoughts are God's thoughts. Specifically, whatever that person thinks becomes a reality in their lives. This is how a righteous mind was created to function, I believe before the fall of man.

I really did not understand this until it first happened to me, then I had to pay attention. One day, I was driving past Sam's Club. I thought, "I need a Sam's Club card." I just thought it, without even speaking it. Unexpectedly, my phone rang and it was my sister calling. She said, "Maxine, I am in Sam's Club and I am getting a card. I decided to put your name down for the second user. So, all you have to do is go into a Sam's Club, show your ID and you will have your card."

I was in amazement because I never talked to my sister about getting a Sam's Club card. I just thought about it before it became a reality. This never happened to me, so I thought maybe it was a coincidence. However, these encounters started happening more frequently.

Another day, I was leaving Walmart and my husband's co-worker came to my thoughts. It was on my heart to buy him and his wife a gift for their baby. As I walked out of Walmart, I ran into this same co-worker.

I would think about someone and the Holy Spirit let me know through my thoughts that I was going to see them. Just recently, I was in the Meeting Place and I had not heard this woman of God on the line for months. I thought about her and as soon as the thought was over, she came on the line. This was supernatural!

I know when I am about to see someone in church I have not seen for a while. My thoughts will stay on that person. The moment that I stepped my foot in church, the person appeared. When these encounters with my thoughts started, I began to realize how powerful my thoughts were. Also, why the enemy tries his best to keep our minds in bondage. After this discovery, I began to see myself delivered from my current situation. Whereas, if I think it, it will show up in my natural world.

Another way intimacy with God makes the believer fruitful is when they constantly sit in the presence of God; His presence causes the believer to walk with a heart of repentance. Our hearts become tender toward God, and we easily repent. When the believer is intimate with God, the flesh is not ruling the person. Their spirit is in control, mastering over the flesh. David is a great example of this! He was not saved, but had a heart of repentance. David lived in the secret place of God.

The prophet Nathan was sent to rebuke David for what he had done to Uriah the Hittite (2 Samuel 12:1–14). David confessed his guilt immediately. David knew what to do when God brought correction to him. He poured his heart out before God and repented for his sins. His heart was made tender living in the presence of God.

Once we are connected to the Vine, believers become prosperous. Prosperity (Hebrew word, *shalowm*, which means completeness, soundness, welfare, and peace) comes from the Lord. When we connect to Him in the secret place there is no lack. An outcome of being in His presence, is everything we touch turns to gold in Him; there is no failure. He takes pleasure in seeing His children prosper (Psalm 35:27). The lives of believers change for the better because fruitfulness is found in the true vine, and apart from Him we can do nothing!

Chapter 15

Intimacy Allows Us to Leave a Legacy

For he issued his laws to Jacob; he gave his instructions to Israel. He commanded our ancestors to teach them to their children, so the next generation might know them—even the children not yet born—and they in turn will teach their own children. So, each generation should set its hope anew on God, not forgetting his glorious miracles and obeying his commands. Then they will not be like their ancestors—stubborn, rebellious, and unfaithful, refusing to give their hearts to God. (Psalm 78:5–8, NLT). These were instructions God gave to the children of Israel. He wanted them to instruct their children in His way, so they would not turn from serving Him. Passing on an inheritance of wonderful acts to the next generation is important to God. This should be important to us, too. God does not want the next generations to forget His mighty wonders. If so, they will become stubborn and rebellious, turning their backs on Him.

When I think about inheritance, I think about my husband's grandmother, Beatrice Ryan. She went to heaven years before Robert and I got married. She left my husband, his siblings, and cousins something they can teach their children and grandchildren today. When we first met, I observed how Robert paid attention to his handwashing and it meant so much to him. A few years later while sitting around the family's table on Christmas, I learned that handwashing was particularly important to his grandmother. She passed on this natural inheritance to Robert and his siblings.

Whether or not they want to pass handwashing to the next generation was up to them.

You may wonder if handwashing is something we can inherit. The answer is yes. His grandmother taught Robert and other family members about the importance of washing their hands. Today, Robert will not eat, sneeze, cough or use the bathroom without washing his hands. This is a simple example of natural inheritance. It sets the stage for what I am about to say. In the natural, I will never get a chance to meet his grandmother, but I know for sure she was a clean and tidy woman. She did not keep it for herself; she passed it on to the next generation.

When I met Pastor Charlene, my sister in Christ, her mother had already gone home to be with the Lord. While on the earth, she was a woman of prayer, wisdom and a classy dresser. In the spirit she had eyes to see and ears to hear. For years, I knew the teachings from Pastor Charlene came directly from her mother. Her mother left such a rich spiritual imprint on her heart. She did not simply keep her mother's rich legacy; she also passed it on to the next generation, her daughter.

Similarly, in my own personal life, my husband and I brought our children up in the Word of God. They knew what it meant to pray, fast, love people, give, attend church, walk in integrity, serve God when it was difficult—and they encountered miracles. We did not only speak about it, they saw it demonstrated through us. When our children were old enough to make choices for themselves, they drew back from the things of God. Sometimes, it seemed as though what we had instilled in them went to waste, but that was not true.

One day, the Lord began to show me little by little that His Word was coming to pass in their lives. My son brought his girlfriend to my home. I went to the door and was surprised to see him get out the car, go over to the passenger's side and open the door for his girlfriend. It shocked me because when he did that, I saw my husband. While growing up, my husband taught him to open the car door for me and my daughter if he could not make it in time. I was overjoyed to see my son practicing what he learned as a child.

In the same way, we taught them how important words are. At times, I thought they did not take me seriously. One day we were having a conversation, my son said to his girlfriend, "I told you, your words are important. I told you speaking negative words is not right!" In shock again, I thought about what the Bible says, *Train up a child in the way he should go: and when he is old, he will not depart from it* (Proverbs 22:6).

The faithfulness of our God to His Word is overwhelming to me. At one point, my son made decisions that were against what we taught him. The enemy told me, "You see, you guys are bad parents. Look at what he is doing." It was a lie. God's Word still came to pass. Even when we are unfaithful, He is a faithful God!

I cannot imagine going home to be with the Lord and not leaving a spiritual and natural legacy for my children and their children to take to another level. When an individual dies without leaving a legacy for another generation, it is sad. The person who died will be easy to forget. Look at the life of Dr. Myles Munroe, his legacy outlived him. He has been deceased for some time now, and the body of Christ everywhere still remembers his great wealth of revelation. Dr. Munroe impacted the body of Christ when he lived on earth. His name will be remembered for centuries.

Also, the body of Christ will never be the same because of Smith Wigglesworth. He was a true demonstration of walking by faith and not by sight. Through his life, the Word of God became flesh. In his ministry, many people received healing; blind eyes were opened, and the dead raised. Smith's name meant something in his time and still today. His descendants should feel honored to be part of his bloodline. The legacy left by Smith Wigglesworth cannot be matched so far, since the world has not met *you* yet! Glory to God!

Can you imagine how sad it would be, if there was no godly altar or legacy left behind by your natural ancestors to take to another level? I recall going to a funeral a couple years ago. By far, it was the saddest funeral I ever attended in my life! The fact that the individual was saved did not help with the sadness I felt. This woman of God died in her wilderness without leaving any godly or natural legacy for her daughter to pass on to future generations. She never discovered the purpose God had deposited on the inside, and died full of destiny.

Regrettably, she will only be remembered for heartache, pain, and suffering left to her family. No person at this funeral knew this woman outside of her twenty-one years of drug addiction. We can still thank God that she was saved and her eternal home was heaven. While sitting at this funeral, my heart broke for this young girl left in a world without her mother to pick up the broken pieces.

I cannot imagine my life without a foundation in Christ Jesus. I would be lost. Just like the young girl whose mother never knew God her entire life. More than likely, she was never taught how to pray. This would have been tragic for me. Looking back over my life, I have been highly favored by God. He brought me through many storms. Surely, if it were not for God's grace and my ancestor's prayers, I would not be here. I thank God that generations before me knew Him and taught me His ways.

The Word of God says, *A good man leaves an inheritance to his children's children* (Proverbs 13:22, NKJV). There is nothing wrong with leaving our children with a great deal of wealth and all of the natural possessions this world has to offer. We should believe God to leave a natural inheritance for our children to change the course of their generation. It is a tragedy if there is no godly altar or inheritance (such as prayer, miracles, signs, and wonders) to take them to another level. The next generation must know how to pray and know how to be a demonstration of mighty wonders. We are responsible for building and passing on a godly legacy to our children. If we do not commit ourselves to building a natural and spiritual inheritance, generations will be lost.

In the book of Jonah, God was going to destroy Nineveh for its wickedness. The children of Israel turned their hearts to God and repented. He changed His mind and Nineveh was saved. When we move over to the book of Nahum, God was angry with Nineveh again. Judgment was released and a whole generation was wiped out. Why were they wiped out? The Israelites backslid; they failed to instruct their children in the things of God, and many turned away from serving Him. They regressed to their wicked ways. If we fail to instruct and pass on a godly inheritance to our children in the Lord while they are growing up—generations after will be lost.

Growing up in my grandmother's home, she instilled prayer and the Word in me. As a child, she sat my brothers and sisters down and made us memorize Scriptures. Because she did, now I have a great love for the Word of God. I am grateful.

Some people think we must scream from a mountaintop to our children to instill the Word of God. The way we live is a demonstration that speaks the most. Our actions tell who a person is better than what we say. In order to build a legacy, time and sacrifices are required.

Someone had a vision of a leader inside a coffin who died with the baton in his hand. Before he died, he did not invest time in anyone's life. There was no one to take his place, he refused to pass on the baton. This is tragic when believers die with their mantle. Instead of positioning and training someone to take over what they had built, they kept it to themselves.

My grandmother positioned her children and grandchildren by demonstrating what she wanted us to be. She built an altar through her constant prayers and fasting. She taught us how to live as born-again believers.

Today, a great number of believers in the faith gleaned testimonies of generals from the past. Listening to those testimonies and miracles built them up. It stirred them to do more and take these testimonies to another level.

Each generation has a responsibility to take the legacy to their generation. In the Old Testament, God kept saying to Israel, do this so that your children will not forget what He brought them out of. As they were about to go into the Promised Land, they had already experienced the mighty acts of God. They saw with their own eyes how the Lord defeated their enemies—to give them victory. He told them to, *commit yourselves wholeheartedly to these words of mine. Tie them to your hands and wear them on your forehead as reminders. Teach them to your children. Talk about them when you are at home and when you are on the road, when you are going to bed and when you are getting up. Write them on the doorposts of your house and your gates, so that as long as the sky remains above the earth, you and your children may flourish in the land the LORD swore to give your ancestors* (Deuteronomy 11:18–21, NLT). God wanted the children to know how important it was to keep His

Word. He wanted them to never forget the miraculous work He performed in the lives of the children of Israel.

As the children of Israel crossed over the Jordan, God told Joshua to build a memorial. He instructed that one man from each tribe pick up one stone from the middle of the Jordan and build a memorial. Why were they building this memorial? *In the future your children will ask you, 'What do these stones mean?' Then, you can tell them, 'They remind us that the Jordan River stopped flowing when the Ark of the LORD's Covenant went across.' These stones will stand as a memorial among the people of Israel forever* (Joshua 4:6–7). God wanted the legacy of the works He had done to go to another generation.

When a generation forgets what God has done, they tend to turn away from Him into sin. Legacies are meant to be carried to another generation, they are not meant to die with the individual. Someone must be available to take up the mantle the same way. Elisha took the mantle of Elijah, along with a double portion of Elijah's spirit. In the Old Testament, I thought it was awesome to learn that Elijah performed fourteen miracles and Elisha performed twenty-eight miracles. This is double portion indeed!

When a believer spends time building an altar of prayer, this intimacy with God must be taken to another generation. Someone must rise up to take the mantle to another level. Before Billy Graham died, he led millions to Christ through his ministry. After he died, a new era began. Someone or many others after him will pick up his mantle of evangelism and take it to another level. Are you the one?

I believe legacies are important. If there is no legacy, then inheritance will be lost and naturally, people will turn away from God. Years ago, when I began building my altar in prayer, my children would say, "Mommy, why you have to be so loud in the morning?" As time went on, when they did not hear me praying, they would ask, "Why was it so quiet this morning? Did you not get up to pray?"

When things went wrong, they would run to me to pray to intercede for them or on behalf of their friends. Sometimes, they would even tell their friends to call their mother and she would pray for them.

One day, my son came home limping from playing basketball after spraining his ankle. He was probably thinking I was going to take him to the hospital (not that I do not believe in doctors). Without even thinking, I laid my hands on his ankle and said, "In the name of Jesus, I speak to this ankle and I command you to be healed!" When I finished, my son had this look on his face like, *Yeah right, Mom.* I said, "Now, I want you to walk on it in Jesus' name. You are healed!" He took a small step on it and began to walk with a slight limp. I said, "God has healed you, by the time you wake up tomorrow morning, there will be no pain all at." He woke up the next day, and the pain was completely gone. Hallelujah!

Another day, my son came home with a friend who was living in his car with his mother and other siblings. They were evicted from their apartment for failing to pay rent. I was led to lay my hands on his friend and prayed that God would intervene. Then, the Holy Spirit laid it in my spirit that they would move into their new place within a week. By faith, I opened my mouth and declared this to the young adult. Within that same week, my daughter who was also friends with that young man came in my room smiling holding the phone.

"Mom, it's the guy you prayed for the other day. He asked me if you were psychic because everything you said and prayed came to pass. They moved into their new apartment and off the street!" Thank you, Jesus! I am not psychic; I am a child of God and I give all the praise to Him!

Maybe you are wondering, what does this have to do with leaving a legacy? I want to tell you, a lot! In order to leave a legacy for the next generation, our children must see demonstration of the One true God living through us. If we tell them our God heals, then they must have an encounter with Jehovah Raphe. If we tell them our God provides, then they must encounter Jehovah Jireh. They must see evidence of Him providing.

There is no pressure to teach and instruct our children, but once they see us living and walking with God—sooner or later they will too. It is literally, doing what Proverbs 22:6 says about training up the child in the way of the Lord. Whining, nagging, and living in fear concerning our children will not bring forth a lasting result. We must believe God to walk in these blessings and power for the sake of our children. They must see a lasting demonstration of our God and how real He is.

Many of you reading this book probably can say, "Sister Maxine, I did not have a praying mother, grandmother or anyone in my family who has left me a godly inheritance. I am the first generation in my family who is serving God." Well, that is no excuse. You must begin today creating a spiritual inheritance before you go to glory and leave your children the mantle. If your children or grandchildren are young and living with you, and you have not gotten started, I want to ask, what you are waiting for? They will learn from your example.

Do not preach one way and live the opposite; this confuses them. They will think it is acceptable to live with one foot in Christ and one foot in the world. Live for God only!

If you have adult children, begin building your prayer altar today. Since we are in a new covenant, altars that are built focus not on the physical, but spiritual. So designate a place, a closet, room, chair, office, corner of a wall, garage, backyard, etc., and make this place your Meeting Place for you and God only. Meet God in this place the same time each day and watch how chains will break off you and the lives of your children.

Remember, God is not unjust and He will *not* forget your labor of love. Claim God's promise over their lives and watch God! Again, it is not wrong to leave money, land, or cars to the next generation. You should. A spiritual inheritance is *more* important. If your children lose all their earthly possessions, they will still know how to get a prayer through, calling on the name of Jesus until something happens. Someone must cultivate a life of intimacy and instruct our children in the way of the Lord. Will it be you?

Will you demonstrate God in the world you live in? Just like the Bible says, so the generation after will not become stubborn, rebellious and they will serve God, and take this rich godly legacy you have built to the generations to come.

Acknowledgements

APOSTLES TONY AND CYNTHIA BRAZELTON, my spiritual parents, I absolutely love you both! I thank God for your relationship with Him. Because of your relationship with God, my life has soared to another dimension in Christ Jesus. You have taught me that I can be me, and your unconditional love for God's people has touched my heart deeply! Your demonstration of love and your passion for God's Word have captivated me and changed my life forever. You both mean more to me than you could ever know! I love you!

Pastor Paula Hazel, your Proverbs 31 lifestyle has captured my heart deeply. Your intimacy with the Father has been an example for me and others to follow. Your love to see God's people live free has been my inspiration. Our relationship means the world to me. I will love you forever.

Pastor Benny Hinn, because of your life of intimacy with God, I have craved more of Him. Thank you for being a powerful demonstration of intimacy and exhibiting God's power.

Prophet Alph Lukau, your prayer life has captured my attention, and your God-given ability to hear and see in the spirit has whet my appetite to see and hear God on another level. I give God praise for your life and thank you for being a demonstration of God's power with no limitation.

Apostle Kenneth Copeland, you have demonstrated what it means to live a life of audacious faith. Your bold risks of faith have been an inspiration to me. Your messages of faith have caused me to believe that there is truly nothing impossible to those who just believe.

Pastor Guillermo Maldonado, your intimate relationship with the one and true living God taught me how to walk in the supernatural power of God, and how to shift every atmosphere that does not line up with the Word of God.

About the Author

When South meets North, you get Maxine A. Ryan arriving on these shores with her prayer altar in hand. Well established as a prayer model and mentor spending time in the secret place, her God-given gift of prayer has enlarged her territory to bring "radical" change to prayer-less lives. Unbeknownst to her, there was a call to ministry drawing her into an *effectual* life of prayer. With a sincere heart to minister to the lost and the found, Maxine has successfully built a lifestyle of intimacy inside the walls of God's presence.

Miraculously healed from a childhood stutter, she speaks the language of heaven fluently with power. With spiritual skill and precision, her prayers can shift *any* atmosphere bringing heaven into the earth—which gives her an edge—for people on the edge. Maxine's ability to reach God in the Throne Room gives her full access to Him on a more personal, passionate and deeper level. This exceptional woman of grace is determined to make sure believers know their spiritual inheritance. Founder of the *Meeting Place,* this intercessor gave birth to her prayer ministry out of an intense desire to serve God. Maxine has authored two other books, *Krazy Faith* and *If You Change Your Words, You'll Change Your Life!*

Wife to husband Robert and mother to Amari and Carisha, Maxine's love for family allows her to pour into the vessels of others. A lifetime student of God's Word, she earned a Bachelor of Arts in Religious Studies from Victory Bible College in Suitland, Maryland. She believes prayer is essential for Christian living. Maxine's passion is intimacy with God and helping God's people grow in their relationship with Him. She has committed her life to discipling others for Christ.

www.ingramcontent.com/pod-product-compliance
Lightning Source LLC
Chambersburg PA
CBHW071855160426
43209CB00005B/1065